## WHAT OTHERS ARE SAYING ABOUT DAVIDE DI GIORGIO AND *BEING UNAPOLOGETIC*

"In *Being Unapologetic*, Davide Di Giorgio charts a path others can follow to find their voices and deliver their messages in an authentic and impactful way. Davide asks only that you unabashedly and unapologetically communicate to those who need your message the most. This book will inspire you to engage the world with your story for positive change. This is the perfect read for anyone on the sidelines needing an inspirational push to be heard."

Brian Tracy
International Best-Selling Author of More Than Seventy Books and Global Speaker

"*Being Unapologetic* is funny, heartfelt, and hopeful. But most of all it's helpful. In a very relatable way, Davide encourages you to ask the right questions, not the popular ones in order to identify your natural gifts, nail down your why, and find your confidence throughout the process. You will be empowered and enlightened by this book and loaded with tools to take your life to the next level."

Katy Temple
Founder & CEO, Katy Temple Media Coaching,
Emmy Award Winning Sportscaster

"This is a must read! Davide shares what he's learned on the front lines of an extraordinary personal and business life. No fluff, no filler—simply the powerful stories, lessons, and practical exercises that will put you on the path to becoming a leader who makes an impact and inspires others."

Charmaine Hammond
CSP, Professional Speaker & Author

"Davide Di Giorgio is the embodiment of life celebrated, and in *Being Unapologetic* he shares the pearls of wisdom and sage insights gained from his journey of self-discovery and empowerment. Davide offers the perspective that we arrived with purpose and simply need to (re)discover that purpose by looking back at who we have been along the way, who we are today, and most importantly, who we need to be going forward. If you want to uncover the truth of who you are, and live a more fulfilling life in doing so, this book will guide you along the path to becoming the best, most authentic version of you."

Mark Lovett
Founder, Storytelling with Impact

"You're in for a treat with *Being Unapologetic*. Few people have figured out how to create their own destinies and go for it like Davide Di Giorgio. As a teacher, accomplished professional speaker, and one of my favorite human beings, Davide Di Giorgio has much to teach all of us. These pages will take you to new heights of success once you begin practicing the tools he so generously offers."

Patrick Snow
Publishing Coach and International
Best-Selling Author of *Creating Your Own Destiny*

"*Being Unapologetic* is more than just another book.... It is a way of thinking, being, and a movement! Through his amazing stories and thoughtful teaching style, Davide raises the bar and sets the example for visionaries, leaders, authors, speakers, and dreamers everywhere. I have had the privilege of attending several of Davide's lively presentations, and his book is just the thing for anyone looking for the inspiration and guidance to elevate their lives to a higher plane!"

Martin K. Fallor, MD, JD
Ophthalmic Plastic Surgeon, Medico-Legal Consultant

"From the very first chapter, I got at least five great ideas of what I could incorporate in my next presentation. I had a smile on my face throughout and could hear Davide's great sense of humor. (Thank you, Davide, for delivering an unboring book!) The principles taught are simple and make so much sense, yet they are very powerful! *Being Unapologetic* is not only a book, it's a movement in which Davide teaches us how to be visionary leaders and speakers. Read it!"

Josée Brisebois
Speaker & Personal Fashion Stylist at WeCanStyle.com

"The first time I saw Davide speak, I was mesmerized at his command of an audience. His unique and gifted command of words carries over into his amazing book, *Being Unapologetic*. This book is vital for visionaries or anyone looking to discover their purpose in life. Whether on stage, in life, or in his book, Davide is the purest example of how living unapologetically is the ultimate path to freedom and a joy-filled life!"

Joshua T. Berglan
Show Host, MC & Dream Designer TheWorldsMayor.com

"As a podcaster, I try very much to help my guests deliver excellent interviews. *Being Unapologetic* does a great job of uncovering many of the teachings and vital 'must haves' you need to be a great interviewer. I always say that being on podcasts is the best place to start to be successful on stages. After reading this book, I have added it to my recommended preparation tools to appear on podcasts. Being polarizing, authentic, and everything that goes with it—all can be found in this book."

Dennis J. Langlais
Host of *The FIVE Minute Bark* Podcast

"Who am I? Why am I? How may I serve? Davide Di Giorgio transforms the reader into a participant in introspection and reflection, leading one to uncover and share those gifts that give purpose. *Being Unapologetic* is for those eager to find their space and place at home, in the workplace, and in the community-at-large."

Brian Tos
Retired Secondary School Teacher

"This book is the grease on the grill that will ignite some fierce flames. Davide Di Giorgio's voice has an unmatched ability to move you, guide you, and shape you…and your future.

"Through a candid and creative platform, Davide manages to connect the 'opportunity dots' not only in his story but also in yours. His book will plug you into the outlet that is your purpose and passion.

"The inspiration from this book will stick to you like a second skin and you'll never be able to shake off its effects.

"Davide is your dashing date to an overdue and well-deserved celebration of you and your journey. Get ready to embrace a version of yourself that you can tweak, perfect, and alter, but never apologize for.

"Davide is masterful at nurturing and empowering his readers/audience in ways that will make them legacies in their own time."

Anthony Zomparelli
Author of *No Fangs Filmore* and *Benvolio's Heart*

"This book is a shortcut on the journey to discovering the best of you. I've learned to surround myself with powerful people who can transform aspects of my own life, and Davide is one of those people. A force for good, he has a special talent to bring out the best in you."

Jeff J. Hunter
The King of Outsourcing

"The wisdom in Davide's book is extremely valuable in helping me review the process around developing my unique message to the world. I am relishing the process of evaluating my own message with the down-to-earth guidance this book gives.

"In *Being Unapologetic*, Davide shares directly from his journey how he discovered his message and how he relays it to the world in an empowering way. His book gives you a strategic framework to develop your own blueprint, one that will help you not only to discover your message and voice, but to share in a way that is authentic and impactful with those you seek to serve, while enabling you to achieve a success that feels fulfilling. Thank you, Davide!"

Anita Narayan
Founder of Breaking Free Unlimited and Be The Inspiration TV

"Please gift yourself and many others with the knowledge in this book!

"I love the breakdown and flow of the chapter layout. Davide really nailed the unfolding of our process of a better knowing and acceptance of ourselves, which leads to more compassion and love for others in our world.

"The exercises are perfectly placed to create immediate shifts in your mindset so you feel more open and free, just being you.

"Don't just use this book as a brilliant way to uplevel your life, but as a life manual! To truly let go and meet the *real* you that is perfect and brilliant...the you we all see and get to experience. The true and beautiful unapologetic *you*!

Nikki Incandela
Visual Branding Photographer and Mentor

"Davide's *Being Unapologetic* is a fresh look at being extraordinary, standing out by being who you are, and finding confidence in the small wins in life. He describes the process of 'celebrating breadcrumbs in your life,' and it is such a great description of what it takes to shine in a world that is so crowded with social media, likes, and selfies. I think deciding to be unapologetic is the only way to go if you want to make meaning in your creative life. A great book for great minds."

Azul Terronez
Author of *The Art of Apprenticeship*

"Davide totally inspires from the moment you meet him, as does his book. *Being Unapologetic* will engage you from the very first word to the very last, inspiring you to find clarity to live life on your terms."

Dylis Guyan
Inspirational Sales and Marketing Leader, Coach and Speaker

"*Being Unapologetic* is all about living your own truth and not letting any obstacles stand in your way. Davide Di Giorgio takes his readers on an inspirational ride through his own journey, and then he brings in the stories of numerous powerful social influencers who have learned to live unapologetically like he has. The result is a book chockful of wisdom from a collection of great minds and admirable people. Don't miss this life-changing book!"

Nicole Gabriel
Author of *Finding Your Inner Truth* and *Stepping into Your Becoming*

"Having Davide come out to work with my students has created a large impact. These students struggle with self-confidence, but in one hour with Davide, there was a noticeable shift in how they perceived themselves. Obviously, this translates in a big way for performing and their commitment to the music, but greater than that, there is a shift that will help them throughout the rest of their lives.

"My teaching philosophy is to teach my students through music, not teach music *to* my students. This has given me an opportunity to better teach my students life skills through music and give them opportunities they would not have otherwise had.

"If anyone is considering having Davide come work with your group—do it! I will be the first to admit I was suspicious, but it was an amazing experience. My kids really enjoyed it and gained quite a bit from it.

"One thing my students have said is that they wished choir was valued on campus. I wanted them to feel valued, so I thought about what choral-wide things could do that. Commissioning a piece means your name is on it forever. With the funds we were gifted through ProjectUNx, we are commissioning some choral works to be performed. It's something not everyone gets to do, so we are having a piece written just for us!"

Robert Davis<br>Choir Director, Ayala High School

"*Being Unapologetic* is a powerful combination of storytelling and mindful integration. Davide shares lessons from life experiences and invites the reader to ask the important questions of life—ultimately facilitating a transformative and empowering experience for anyone who picks up this book."

Mike Sherbakov<br>Founder, Greatness Foundation, MikeSherbakov.com

"Davide Di Giorgio has a message for the ages. In *Being Unapologetic*, he reveals how we can all work through our fears and deepest insecurities to shine our beacon to all the world, help our fellow human beings, quit apologizing for the wonderful beings we are, and create the life we've always dreamed of. I ate up every word, and then went back and read it again. This one's a keeper."

Tyler R. Tichelaar, PhD<br>Award-Winning Author of *Narrow Lives*, *The Best Place*, and *When Teddy Came to Town*

"Davide Di Giorgio has created such a wonderful system for self-growth and development. Most authors push your focus entirely to the future. Davide asks you to look back to your earliest years and rediscover who you truly are. He then guides the reader through planning a future that supports who he or she is, unapologetically."

Michael Beauclerc
Co-Founder/Executive Director of the Canadian Drumline Association

"True wealth lies in a person's story; telling it in a way to transform others and create personal freedom is a craft. Davide Di Giorgio has mastered it and has now crafted a true instructional vessel to teach the masses to do the same. No doubt the lives who take hold of this tool and use it accordingly will experience a transformation that will awaken a new level of success and fulfillment. Written with excellence, timed to perfection, with an undeniable mix of humor and heart, this one is one for the record books. Dive in; your true wealth awaits you."

Danelle Delgado
CEO Life Intended, World-Renowned Speaker & High-Performance Business Strategist

If you're ready to positively transform your life, then read and absorb the strategies in this brilliant book by my friend Davide Di Giorgio! Davide is an amazing speaker and coach who truly cares about helping others and his ideas will make a positive difference in your life!

James Malinchak
Featured on ABCs Hit TV Show, *Secret Millionaire*
Authored 20 Books, Delivered 3,000 Presentations & 1,000 Consultations, Best-Selling Author, Millionaire Success Secrets
Founder, www.MillionaireFreeBook.com

# BEING UNAPOLOGETIC

EMPOWERING YOU TO BECOME AN INFLUENTIAL SPEAKER AND VISIONARY LEADER

## DAVIDE DI GIORGIO

AVIVA
PUBLISHING
New York

**BEING UNAPOLOGETIC:**
**Empowering You to Become an Influential Speaker and Visionary Leader**

© 2018 by Davide Di Giorgio. All rights reserved.

Published by:
Aviva Publishing
Lake Placid, NY
(518) 523.1320
AvivaPubs.com

All Rights Reserved. No part of this book may be used or reproduced in any manner whatsoever without the expressed written permission of the author. Address all inquiries to:

Davide Di Giorgio
Telephone: (619) 363.0568
Email: Davide@BeingUnapologetic.com
BeingUnapologetic.com
BeingUnapologeticTV.com

Hardcover ISBN: 978-1-947937-54-3
Paperback ISBN: 978-1-947937-56-7
Library of Congress Control Number: 2018908082

Editor: Tyler Tichelaar/Superior Book Productions
Cover Design: Nicole Gabriel/AngelDog Productions
Interior Book Layout: Nicole Gabriel/AngelDog Productions
Chapter Graphics: Adam Bartanus
Cover Photo: John Antezana/Caliphoto Dreamin Photography
Author Photo: Nikki Incandela/Nikki Incandela Photography

Every attempt has been made to source properly all quotes.

Printed in the United States of America

First Edition

2 4 6 8 10 12

# DEDICATION

To my mentor, friend, and greatest teacher, Fredrick H. Thury (1945–2006): While you were teaching me how to become a successful musical director and theater producer, you actually taught me how to be me. Your greatest gift was the ability to see possibility in others and support people in bringing that possibility into the light. Not only did you bring out the best in me, but you taught me how to do the same for others. This book is a testament to your legacy, and now my legacy for the world. I did it, Fred! I finally wrote a book, just like you told me to. Until we are together again for the first time in the great beyond, I will continue to carry on the legacy of *being* you gifted to me.

To my American parents, Anita and Pete: Thank you for seeing me for who I am when I didn't know it myself. Thank you for your unconditional love. Thank you for helping me redefine *family* and feel like I belong. I love you both and I wish for you to continue to live all the days of your lives with unprecedented celebration and love.

To Heath, my husband: This book would not have been possible without your unselfish support and love. Thank you for giving me the space and time to grow my wings. Thank you for being who you are, unapologetically, and for honoring who I am as we continue to build our lives together. Oh, the adventures we will have! Love you, babe.

# ACKNOWLEDGMENTS

To the heroes who show me what it looks like to think, act, and be unapologetic:

Jesse Alberta, Christina Aguilera, Baron Baptiste, P. T. Barnum, Richard Branson, Brené Brown, Jesus, Jack Canfield, Kathy Cates, Cher, Martha Couto, Simon Cowell, Kendra Dahlstrom, Anna Danes, Leonardo DaVinci, Stephen Dela Cruz, Ellen DeGeneres, Celine Dion, Walt Disney, Wayne Dyer, Kelly Earp, Galileo Galiliei, Bill Gates, Katharine Gladwish, Sean Gorman, Joseph Haydn, Jake Heilbrunn, Abraham-Hicks, Michael Jackson, Steve Jobs, Daymond John, Fran Kick, Craig Kielburger, Barb LaPlante, James Malinchak, Ricky Martin, Joseph McClendon III, Donna McEvoy, Matthew Morrison, Jason Mraz, Elon Musk, Lisa Nichols, Benj Pasek, Dolly Parton, Justin Paul, Katy Perry, Vidya Reddy, Dr. Andrzej Rozbicki, Stephen Sondheim, Simon Sinek, Kasha Slavner, Meryl Streep, Mother Teresa, Justin Timberlake, Brian Tracy, Michael Tracy, Mark Twain, Megan Unsworth, Andrew Lloyd Webber, Eric Whitacre, and Oprah Winfrey.

To those who took the time to review and endorse this book. Your beautiful words have given me the confidence to soar! Michael Beauclerc, Joshua T. Berglan, Josée Brisebois, Danelle Delgado, Martin K. Fallor, Dylis Guyan, Charmaine Hammond, Jeff J. Hunter, Dennis Langlais, Mark Lovett, Anita Narayan, Rhodes Perry, Mike Sherbakov, Katy Temple, Azul Terrones, Brian Tos, and Anthony Zomparelli.

Unapologetic Influencers: without you this book would not be as rich. Thank you for sharing who you are. Sarah-Nada Arfa, Cindy Ashton, Heather Joy Bassett, Joie Cheng, Carson Cooper, Carmenza David, Casey Nicole Fox, Christine Gail, Kat Halushka, Milana Leshinsky, Niraj Mendis, LaKeisha Michelle, Randy Molland, Re Perez, Christine Rosas, Vanessa Shaw, Nick Unsworth, and Brian K. Wright.

Heartfelt thanks to Robert Davis and the students of the Ruben S. Ayala High School Choir for opening their classroom and trusting my vision for them. I can't wait to give you the standing ovation you deserve when you premier your newly commissioned choral work.

Thank you to Deanne Goodman and Jensen Scherer for helping me to bring Project UNx to life.

To my biggest supporters who contributed to making this book and the bigger vision come to life. Thank you for believing in me. I will always cherish your generosity and love. Jenn Beninger, Christopher Cailler, Claudia Carrillo, Long Le, Dorci Leissner-Hill.

To my extended American family who've loved me and believed in me even when becoming a resident was just a crazy dream: Kelly Earp and Catie Watson, Miranda and Nick Gilfillan, Guillermo Suero and Joseph Max Sánchez, Travis, Sara, and Barlow Holley, Virginia Kittredge, and Mary Pollard.

Thank you to my bullies who made me who I am today.

Johnny Antezana: Thank you for capturing the incredible moment on fire that has become the cover of this book.

Patrick Snow: Thank you for your mentorship and your friendship. Thank you for seeing the story in me and empowering me to become the influential speaker and visionary leader I am today.

# CONTENTS

**CELEBRATION**     20

Foreword by Patrick Snow     23
Introduction: It All Begins With Celebration     27

**PART I: DISCOVERING YOUR PURPOSE**     31

| | | |
|---|---|---|
| Chapter 1: | Uncovering the Truth | 33 |
| Spotlight: | Unapologetic Influencer | |
| | Unbroken by Christine Rosas | 41 |
| Chapter 2: | Asking Better Questions | 45 |
| Spotlight: | Unapologetic Influencer | |
| | Unchained by Carson Cooper | 55 |
| Chapter 3: | Accepting Yourself | 61 |
| Spotlight: | Unapologetic Influencer | |
| | Unloved by Re Perez | 68 |
| Chapter 4: | Acting Courageously | 71 |
| Spotlight: | Unapologetic Influencer | |
| | Unafraid by Niraj Mendis | 79 |
| Chapter 5: | Letting Go | 83 |
| Spotlight: | Unapologetic Influencer | |
| | Unburdened by Heather Joy Bassett | 95 |
| Chapter 6: | Going All In | 99 |
| Spotlight: | Unapologetic Influencer | |
| | Unleashed by Christine Gail | 109 |

| Chapter 7: | Knowing You Are Already Enough | 113 |
| Spotlight: | Unapologetic Influencer | |
| | Unbeatable by Randy Molland | 121 |

## PART II: DEVELOPING YOUR LEADERSHIP SKILLS — 125

| Chapter 8: | Accountability | 127 |
| Spotlight: | Unapologetic Influencer | |
| | Unbreakable by Kat Halushka | 137 |
| Chapter 9: | Embracing Different as Normal | 141 |
| Spotlight: | Unapologetic Influencer | |
| | Unconventional by Milana Leshinsky | 151 |
| Chapter 10: | Taking a Stand | 155 |
| Spotlight: | Unapologetic Influencer | |
| | Unmessable by Casey Nicole Fox | 166 |
| Chapter 11: | Storytelling | 171 |
| Spotlight: | Unapologetic Influencer | |
| | Uncorked by Cindy Ashton | 185 |
| Chapter 12: | Having Faith | 191 |
| Spotlight: | Unapologetic Influencer | |
| | Unwavering by Nick Unsworth | 202 |

## PART III: DELIVERING YOUR VISION — 205

| Chapter 13: | Speaking Your Truth | 207 |
| Spotlight: | Unapologetic Influencer | |
| | Unquiet by Carmenza David | 212 |
| Chapter 14: | Showing Up and Making a Statement | 215 |
| Spotlight: | Unapologetic Influencer | |
| | Unboring by Vanessa Shaw | 223 |

| | | |
|---|---|---|
| Chapter 15: | Becoming Unforgettable | 227 |
| Spotlight: | Unapologetic Influencer | |
| | Unforgettable by Joie Cheng, MSW | 238 |
| Chapter 16: | Measuring Your Value | 243 |
| Spotlight: | Unapologetic Influencer | |
| | Unorthodox by Sarah-Nada Arfa | 252 |
| Chapter 17: | Leading With Vision | 257 |
| Spotlight: | Unapologetic Influencer | |
| | Unreasonable by Brian K. Wright | 265 |
| Chapter 18: | Being Unstoppable | 271 |
| Spotlight: | Unapologetic Influencer | |
| | Unapologetic by LaKeisha Michelle | 276 |

## CELEBRATION 279

| | |
|---|---|
| A Final Note: Who Are You Being? | 281 |
| About the Author | 287 |
| Project Being Unapologetic | 289 |
| Speaker and Influencer Coaching | |
| Being Unapologetic Experiences | 291 |
| Additional Resources | 295 |
| Book Davide to Speak | 297 |

"No one ever made a difference by being like everyone else."

— P. T. Barnum

# CELEBRATION
## WHAT ARE YOU CELEBRATING RIGHT NOW?

# FOREWORD
## BY PATRICK SNOW

Bravo!

Every now and then, I stumble across a book that forever changes my life. A book I will cherish always and let no one else borrow from fear it won't be returned. *Being Unapologetic* is one of those books, and it certainly will be a classic in the decades to come! So if you are standing in a bookstore reading this foreword and contemplating buying this book, my best advice to you is to *buy this book now* or forever live a life of regret!

For as long as I can remember, I have lived by the adage that it is better just to "do something first without asking for permission, and then apologize later" (if needed). I also have lived by the philosophy for years that "Leadership is not given; it is taken!" To me, that is what being unapologetic is all about, and it's exactly the way Davide Di Giorgio and the others featured in this book have lived their lives, and hence, their massive success should not surprise you!

Davide Di Giorgio certainly is unapologetic in every aspect of his life. But more importantly, he is one of the most authentic, genuine, and warm-hearted people I know, and I am honored to call him my friend! He is truly one of my favorite people on this planet, and I am honored to write this foreword and support this project as his publishing coach.

I believe successful people live their lives being unapologetic. They live by the advice of Les Brown: "Never let someone else's opinion of you determine your reality." I would take it a step further and add: Never let someone else's opinion of you stop you!

You see, successful people are rule breakers; they are unapologetic; they do what is right even if it is not popular or what the majority of people would do. This mindset, which you will learn in this book, is exactly the opposite of what we are taught in school: Don't speak up. Don't get out of line. Play it safe. Get a good education so you can find a solid job. I believe if you follow this advice, you will eventually be apologizing to your family for losing your job, and then you will be begging the unapologetic entrepreneurs for a job.

I believe being unapologetic means following your passions, not seeking permission from others, doing what you love, serving others, living on your own terms while still solving a need in the marketplace, and serving others to make the world a better place!

Furthermore, as you develop this mindset, you will achieve what this book's subtitle promises: Empowering high achievers to be visionary leaders and successful speakers. Additionally, I believe you will achieve your freedom and get what we all want, which is more time, more money, more health, more love, and more happiness in life.

In this powerful book, you will learn how to discover the leader within and be empowered to build a leadership platform and a movement based on who you are being (and who you've always been). You will learn what it truly means to be courageous in order to bring a vision or dream to life. You will overcome personal limiting beliefs that are keeping you from achieving the success for which you are destined. You will learn why starting with "why" could actually be stalling you from your biggest success.

Furthermore, you will develop the accountability to achieve personal and business success. You will learn how to uncover your true identity and worth. You will develop the discipline and confidence of a visionary speaker and leader—one who dares to challenge the "status quo" and create lasting positive impact for the world and others. You will take on the attitude of champions. You will learn how to lead with vision, as opposed to value, so you can exponentially increase results and deepen relationships. And finally, you will be able to deliver your story, message, and vision unapologetically and successfully so you can radically inspire others into action and positive transformation.

# FOREWORD

In these pages, Davide Di Giorgio will provide you with the knowledge, skill set, and confidence to live your life the way you have always desired without having to seek approval from others. Your heart and soul will shine, your energy levels will soar, and your success will be like nothing you have ever experienced!

When you follow the formulas and strategies in this book, your whole life will change. You will be asked to speak at huge conferences, your coaching practice will skyrocket, you will travel the world in service to others, and you will achieve internal solitude and peace of mind. Most importantly, you will be living true to the destiny for which you were born. You will blaze your own trail for others to follow, and your example, mentoring, and new way of life will impact thousands of others also to live with authenticity.

Throughout this book, you will learn that you are the driving force for you to take the leadership role in your life, to never again ask for permission, and to live life on your own terms. You will achieve all of the career, family, and wealth goals you desire. Most importantly, you will become a servant leader, making the world a better place for generations to come.

So get ready for an amazing ride. Buckle your seatbelt and prepare yourself for a life-changing experience like no other, that will bring you fulfillment, contentment, peace, and most importantly, a life in which you never ask anyone again for permission!

Respectfully,

Patrick Snow

Publishing Coach, Professional Speaker, and International Best-Selling Author of *Creating Your Own Destiny*, *The Affluent Entrepreneur*, and *Boy Entrepreneur*

PatrickSnow.com
ThePublishingDoctor.com

**UN** ARE YOU READY TO BE
UNAPOLOGETIC?

# INTRODUCTION
## IT ALL STARTS WITH CELEBRATION

"Find out who you are and be that person. That's what your soul was put on this Earth to be. Find that truth, live that truth, and everything else will come."

— Ellen DeGeneres

Which of these statements ever crosses your mind?

You're not good enough! Who do you think you are? You don't have that X factor! What if you fail? What if they think you're a fraud? What if you succeed? You'll never really make it! That's just a dream! If only I could get a break like they did!

As a result, do you find yourself playing small? Do you sometimes not share your ideas for fear of being judged? Are you waiting for that great idea or opportunity that will be the one? Do you believe you're here on this earth for a bigger purpose? Do you feel like you've put in the time but still can't get a break? Are you constantly *delivering* and *adding value* but still feel like you can't get ahead?

I know what it's like. I've spent nearly my entire life playing a smaller game than I knew I could. I've spent my entire life waiting for others, the right moment, the right opportunity, the right way to say it, the right partners…. And it's exhausting. I know what it feels like to spend your entire life feeling like you're apologizing for who you are, or diminishing your light so as not to outshine everyone around you, even though you've known your entire life that you naturally shine bright and have the potential for great things!

In this book, you'll discover the truth about yourself so you can truly begin to accept and celebrate who you already are and how to go *all in* on your dreams and vision. You'll develop the confidence and critical thinking skills that will allow you to take a stand for what you believe and how to enroll others through your story. You'll learn how to share your gifts with the world and to lead others with vision instead of playing the *value game* where it feels as though you're always chasing others *and* your dreams.

I'm going to teach you how to uncover and unleash the X factor that will allow you to achieve your mission and vision just like the world's greatest personalities, leaders, speakers, and influencers!

If you apply the lessons, techniques, and wisdom shared in this book, and you commit to being accountable to daily discovery and celebration, then you will not only become the visionary leader and speaker you desire to become, but you will also rediscover your true purpose and passion for life. It's up to you to glean the lessons and apply them to your life, and to be committed to the process and practice of being unapologetic, unmessable, unstoppable…and beyond.

For over twenty-five years, I've worked with and studied performers, speakers, leaders, and visionaries across multiple industries as a composer, musical director, producer, educator, and business owner. The performing arts were my training grounds. Think about it—in musical theater, performers are required to sing abstract lyrics that bring characters and ideas to life that move audiences and command standing ovations. I discovered the secrets to moving audiences and people into inspired action. I developed a way to get the best out of people who have a big mission and vision for others. At the same time, it's a lifelong, ongoing study and discovery process. My commitment is to you—the on-purpose, high achiever who is up to something bigger. I've committed my life to supporting others to bring big ideas to life, and this book represents the culmination of my life's work.

# INTRODUCTION

Dreamers, visionaries, and trailblazers—high achievers like you—don't always have an easy go at things. I get it. I've been there. I'm still there at times. It may feel as though your ideas are too big. That your vision is so big that others just don't see it. Even your friends and family may, at times, encourage you to choose a more traveled path. And I understand you've been at this a long time. You've had a vision for a long time, and it may feel like you've spent your whole life already trying to bring it to fruition. I understand, and I want you to know that I see what's possible for you. I believe the world is waiting for you and your message, and I know you are the only person who can bring your idea to the world.

I see the miracle you are and the power you possess to radically transform and bless the world with your gifts. Take a moment to look at the cover image of this book. I want you to imagine yourself on that stage, confetti blowing by you as the audience cheers you on. They are celebrating you. I am celebrating you in each chapter of this book, and every step of the way. I want you to lean on me when you think you can't make it. I'll be your cheerleader, mentor, and resource that you can look to as you create and catalyze your own movement.

This book is divided into three major parts: Discovering Your Purpose, Developing Your Leadership Skills, and Delivering Your Vision. You will notice that a section on Celebration begins and ends the book. Why? Celebration has become the single most powerful skill I've used for personal transformation and the transformation of thousands I've worked with. You will be encouraged to celebrate throughout the book.

The book is designed to do exactly what the subtitle states: to empower you to become a visionary leader and speaker, and it is laid out to take you through a process of (re)discovery, development, and finally delivery and celebration of who you are and what your vision, mission, and message is for this world.

A special word about, "I don't know" and "I'm not ready":

You will never be ready, and you will never fully know. (How's that for an unapologetic nudge?)

At any point during your journey through this book, if you are faced with a question you can't answer or you get the feeling of being overwhelmed, I encourage you to apply this line of thinking:

Replace "I don't know" with "If I did know, the answer would be...."

Replace "I'm not ready" with "If I were ready, the answer/next step would be...."

Replace "I'm feeling overwhelmed" with "If I weren't feeling overwhelmed, the answer/next step would be...."

At the end of each chapter, you'll find a spotlight feature for what I call Unapologetic Influencers. These extraordinary coaches, entrepreneurs, business owners, and leaders share their stories and the lessons they've learned along the way through the lens of an *un-* word of their choice. They believe, unapologetically, in their visions and their missions. It is my hope that their stories will inspire you also to step into the spotlight to declare your mission and message to the world, unapologetically.

You are closer than you think to becoming a visionary leader and speaker. Are you ready? Are you ready to discover, develop, and deliver your idea worth spreading, your vision, and to build your on-fire movement? Are you ready to stretch and grow your vision and your comfort zone and step into a new reality? Are you ready to live out your purpose and, in turn, inspire others to do the same? Are you ready to become the visionary leader and speaker I see inside you? If so...great, let's begin the journey together. You're ready, now, to begin the journey to unapologetic you!

Davide Di Giorgio

# PART I
# DISCOVERING YOUR PURPOSE

# UN ARE YOU READY TO BE UNBROKEN?

# UNCOVERING THE TRUTH

"If you enter this world knowing you are loved and you leave this world knowing the same, then everything that happens in between can be dealt with."

— Michael Jackson

Life begins with celebration.

Even before you arrive, at the moment of finding out a new baby is coming, there is celebration.

My love for making a statement began early in life, and in my grand style, I decided to arrive a little early, in the middle of a Saturday night during a perfectly half-full moon.

As the story goes, upon my arrival, the delivery room nurse exclaimed, "This one's going to be a piano player!" While this statement challenged my immigrant parents, who had neither an affinity for music nor the belief that music was a viable life option for their son, they celebrated my arrival with much love.

At every step of the way and with every life milestone, there is celebration.

Early life is a series of celebrations. The first smile, first laugh, first words, and of course, the first steps—each moment is met with a celebration and each celebration reinforces the truth of who you are.

Along the way, there are defining moments that reveal your character and talents.

I've always been a morning person—at times, to my parents' frustration. I had a knack for getting up early and getting myself into, shall we say, adventure.

I have a vague memory (confirmed by my mother) of getting up early one morning to collect two dozen eggs and a tub of ricotta cheese from the refrigerator. It seems I showed early talent for creativity in the kitchen, though in this case, my ingredients and I ended up on the living room carpet, where I decided to create my first culinary delight.

While there was no immediate celebration in this situation (rather, quite the contrary), Mom eventually took on an "If you can't beat 'em, join 'em" approach. Despite creating a mini-disaster on the living room floor, I had shown my talent and interest for cooking. This began a Sunday morning tradition of me sitting at the kitchen table watching (and sometimes assisting) Mom as she prepared food for the week.

It was a weekly celebration; in fact, one I very much looked forward to well into my teens.

Discovering the truth of who you are doesn't always come with a celebration. Sometimes, it's just one of those things that comes out when you're pressed to solve a problem and left to your own devices.

When I was in junior kindergarten (Canadian schooling at the time started two years before first grade, with junior and senior kindergarten, respectively), I had quite the fan club of girlfriends. I was the classroom pick for playing "house" and "doctor" so much so that the girls would end up fighting over me.

Never being one for conflict, one day, I set out to resolve this mounting drama.

When the teacher had stepped out of the classroom for a moment, I moved into action. First, I sent the other boys off to play with their cars and trucks. Then I asked the girls to line up beside each other as I pulled up a chair and stood on it in front of them.

I proceeded to declare, "Andrea, you're going to be on Monday! Ezra, you'll get Tuesday! Sonia, you will be Wednesday...and Thursday!" (Sonia was my favorite; she, incidentally, became my girlfriend in third grade for probably at least a few minutes.)

In this moment of leadership, I learned several things about myself and the power of being me:

1. Having a clear outcome in mind (what I call vision today) moved me to take bold action and awakened a confidence in me that I didn't know was there.

2. Vision aroused a leader within me.

3. When I acted as the leader I was born to be (simply being me, unapologetically), others followed.

Think back to your own childhood. What moments can you identify when you acted from who you truly are, without filter?

_____
_____
_____
_____
_____
_____
_____
_____

Based on these moments, what is your truth? Position it below as an "I am" statement.

For example, based on my kindergarten girlfriend scenario, I would say, "I am a popular, well-liked, creative problem solver and confident leader."

_____

_____

_____

_____

## THE REAL TRUTH

Steve Jobs once said, "You can't connect the dots looking forward; you can only connect them looking backwards. So, you have to trust that the dots will somehow connect in your future. You have to trust in something—your gut, destiny, life, karma, whatever."

So many people are on missions to discover their life purposes by projecting into the future, laying out plans, creating vision boards, hiring life coaches, and exploring spiritual practices—all forward looking activities.

The truth is that you aren't here on this earth to discover your purpose. You arrived with purpose, and if you pay attention to the moments in your life when you acted from who you truly are, you'll recognize that purpose.

The truth, then, exists in what you've already done and, more importantly, who you've already shown up as.

When I work with leaders and speakers, the first phase I have them explore is always the discovery of who they've already been their entire lives.

# UNCOVERING THE TRUTH

You see, you've been dropping breadcrumbs since you arrived. Since that first standing ovation at the moment of your birth, there have been moments when you have shown up as you. Just like I did with my kindergarten and ricotta-and-eggs-on-the-carpet moments. It's in those moments that your truth and purpose are revealed.

## WHO ARE YOU?

Your purpose shows up in who you are. Why you do what you do is because of who you are (and who you've always been).

Think back to your early years, even the years that you yourself can't remember, to imagine how much you were celebrated for who you were in any given moment.

With each celebration, you gained confidence and reinforced your identity. Every time you were celebrated for smiling, laughing, taking a step, going potty—regardless of how small of a celebration—you stepped further into your being, and you did it *un*apologetically! In fact, you were encouraged to be unapologetically you. Silly, joyful, playful, creative, inquisitive...you.

So, what changed?

I believe the change came when you forgot the truth of who you are—a miracle—and you stopped celebrating that simple fact.

Somewhere along the way, you were encouraged less to *be* who you are and more to mold to societal norms and expectations. You were asked to be quiet, to act appropriately, and, ultimately, to diminish your light so as not to stick out or be different.

What a shame. The truth is you are different, and the more you can accept and celebrate that in your difference exists your truth, your purpose, your message, and your miracle, the more you'll be able to live out your truth and miracle, abundantly.

## FINDING YOUR WAY BACK TO YOU—EXTRAORDINARY YOU

How do you rediscover who you are if you feel like you've lost your way? How do you embrace being unapologetically you?

It all starts with recognizing and celebrating the breadcrumbs of your life. The breadcrumbs are the stories and incidents that make up your life—from birth to the present.

Every new client I work with goes through this process, from seasoned speaker to teenage leader.

I call this process the *Everyday Extraordinary Storytelling Book*, and it's designed to expose who you are through whom you've always been.

Look back on your life and begin to document all the stories you remember. For the purpose of this exercise, I define stories as incidents. Think of it in terms of "The time when…" situations that you remember. They could be good memories or bad memories; everything counts, and everything reveals some aspect of your being. Your work is simply to document via brain-dump every incident you remember, no matter how insignificant it may seem to you.

The trick is not to apply any filter on the incident itself; simply document everything you remember as you remember it, with a few words that will jog your memory of the incident itself.

To illustrate, I had a client who went through the process and warned me that she had included several inane memories, one of which had to do with how well she brushed her teeth.

For me, this simple incident revealed that she was detail-oriented, so I asked her questions about how her attention to detail had run her life. She was shocked. You show up in your life, everywhere! The breadcrumbs will reveal themselves.

Although my parents didn't know it at the time, I would ultimately show my talent for music in a big way. The nurse was right. And it has been in the moments when I have operated from my true north, unapologetic me, that miracles have happened for me and for others.

It's taken me over forty years to come to this realization and understanding of my identity and the truth of who I am. Now, I'm on a mission to empower you to step into your own miracle sooner, rather than later—in fact, right now.

## YOUR *EVERYDAY EXTRAORDINARY STORYTELLING BOOK* (AND LIFE!)

As you may have guessed, the *Everyday Extraordinary Storytelling Book* is not something you will ever complete. It will become a practice—a way to see the world and see how you interact within it. New past memories will continue to come up as you journey on through life. I suggest you get a special journal that you can add to for years to come. Or start a digital notebook. I use a tool called Evernote where I continually add stories that ultimately become new ideas and content for future keynote talks, social media posts and videos, and even books.

Begin to document the stories of your life in your own *Everyday Extraordinary Storytelling Book* to start the process of peeling back the layers of who you truly are.

Take a few minutes right now to fill the space below to get you started.

Remember, this is a brain dump, so everything counts and belongs that you remember.

_____

_____

_____

_____

_____

As Michael Jackson states in the opening quote of this chapter, everything between the two finite standing ovation moments in your life (life and death) is simply a matter of living. I've come to celebrate all those moments as the clues to who we truly are.

Celebration matters. What are you celebrating right now?

_____

_____

_____

# SPOTLIGHT: UNAPOLOGETIC INFLUENCER

## UNBROKEN
### BY CHRISTINE ROSAS

*Christine Rosas is a speaker, teacher, and inner voice enthusiast.*

For me, being unbroken means being aware that you are okay, right now, just as you are showing up in this moment. While there may be an awareness within you that parts of your personality or your situation could use a tweak or maybe a large overhaul, this awareness is gentle. There's no sense of urgency to fix anything. Instead, there is a deeper knowing of one simple step you can take, and then another, all the way to your intended goal.

When you live your life unbroken, you do not act with a sense of shame for who you are. If you need to cry, you allow your tears to flow. If you need to laugh, you do it loud. If you happen to shout in anger, you honor yourself and those involved with a sense of grace. You acknowledge your contribution to a challenging situation. All of these acts represent moments in your life. They are not the full expression of who you are.

When you accept that you are unbroken, you realize there is nothing to fix. You then let go of the sense of urgency to be someone else. If you want to be unbroken, do not waste your energy on being someone other than who you are right now. Instead, gain the courage to sit with the version of you right now. Honor this version of you by witnessing it.

In a perfect world, everyone would see everyone else as unbroken. However, we live in a world of people who have had their own life experiences that have created their own perspectives on various situations. Consequently, you may have a moment in which another judges you as broken. My hope is that you take a moment to place your hand on your heart, close your eyes, and breathe deeply. Focus your attention on your heart, the place that holds what truly represents you. Feel into who you truly are. Allow this moment of acknowledging your true self to overshadow others' judgment.

Let me now share with you a story of how I live unbroken. When my two kids and I moved back to the United States, my husband stayed behind for a few months to continue working in Saudi Arabia. We reunited for a vacation in a house along the Washington coast. It was a beautiful way to celebrate my birthday. However, instead of enjoying the gorgeous view through the panoramic windows in the living room, I found myself, once again, in the bathroom shower, curled up in a fetal position and sobbing. This was so typical of me. Everyone was excited to be reunited as a family, yet I was snippy and wished to be somewhere else, so I hid behind the excuse of needing a shower to get away.

I allowed a strain of thoughts to lead me right down the spiral of shame. *Why do I yell so much at my kids? Why do I feel so exhausted? I want to feel happier and enjoy this time with my husband. I need to be a better wife. I need to be a better mom. Why do I always get like this when everyone else is happy? What's wrong with me?*

I felt like I knew better than to feel this way. I put in my time in therapy. I read all the popular self-help books. I knew what to do: think happy thoughts, write the gratitude lists, look around and see how lucky I am, for goodness sake. But I couldn't. I felt hopeless. All this doing, and look at me: a broken mess on the shower floor. I kept sobbing, repeating to myself, "When will this ever stop? When will this ever stop!"

Then it occurred to me. All this doing. Where was it leading me? Where did I intend to go? If I were truly honest with myself, I wanted to escape to a better version of me. I was mentally running as fast as I could to be somewhere and someone else.

Then another deeper shift occurred and I thought, *What would happen if I actually spent time with the me of this moment? What if I honored her? What if I held her and let her know she is okay? What would that look like?*

As I chose to stay on that shower floor, acknowledging, listening, and honoring the me of that moment, that heavy cloud of burden—the need to do and be more—lifted. I was able to see possibilities of enjoyment in that moment. Sure, I was still a bit worn out from my current situation. But I felt hope, gratitude, and peace, and without the trudging to "get back on track."

In that moment, I realized life is messy. It's full of moments in which we are a divine expression of our true self, and other moments in which we are challenged by life. Yet none of these moments are a sign that we are broken.

When we feel broken and like a failure, we take the advice of others as law. Our inner voice no longer matters. When someone else's opinion differs from what we hold in our heart, we see that as more proof that we don't know what's best for us.

I lived this way for the majority of my life. If I had not chosen to allow all of me to be as it was in each moment, I would still be second-guessing the power of my inner guidance system.

Trust your inner guidance system. Believe that you, too, are unbroken. You'll find that life not only gets easier, but you can then embrace your true you.

**UN** ARE YOU READY TO BE
UNCHAINED?

# ASKING BETTER QUESTIONS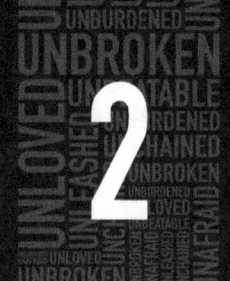

"Stop trying to fix yourself, and be yourself."

— Baron Baptiste

In the first chapter, you began the process of unearthing your true essence: not only who you are, but who you've been your entire life. The person you arrived as at birth. The person who is a born leader, the product of a miracle, and in turn, a miracle maker.

In looking at the clues you've left since your arrival, you may begin to see how you've shown up throughout your life. The *Everyday Fxtraordinary Storytelling Book* process reveals you through your everyday actions, interactions, and incidents.

In this chapter, I am going to challenge you to stop asking the wrong questions when it comes to your purpose and who you are.

## BREADCRUMBS

I imagine it's not by accident that my role in life has often been that of the guide.

When I was in sixth grade, my school got a new vocal music teacher. When this teacher announced she was going to start a new choir, I was elated!

By this time, I had already lived up to my delivery room nurse's prophecy. At about the age of six, I had started showing a real talent for music. My father had brought home a small electric piano keyboard—the Bontempi. I can still see it my mind! It had no more than eighteen keys and came with an accompanying music book.

Within hours of its arrival, I was studying and creating, much to my parents' amazement (or maybe horror, because I think what went on in their minds was, *Oh, no! This means we may have to invest in music lessons and, one day, a piano!* (Incidentally, in sixth grade, I did finally convince my parents to buy me an upright piano!)

In second grade, I auditioned for a highly celebrated choir school for boys. At about the same time, I had taken a deep interest in some of the great composers and had read through Beethoven's biography for pleasure.

So when the new school choir was announced, I was ready!

I'll never forget showing up to the auditions at lunch. I knew I had it in the bag, having spent some time already getting in the good books with Mrs. LaPlante (the choir teacher). I really liked her, and she put a lot of work in for us kids.

At the end of the auditions, I was smiling from ear to ear. Mrs. LaPlante pulled me aside and said, "Davide, I'd love you to be part of the choir [Yes!] as our accompanist!" What?

She went on to explain that I was far too talented to be just a member of the choir...that I showed great talent as a leader. And so, at twelve, I became the youngest accompanist in my district. For the next few years, I accompanied the choir at festivals, competitions, and concerts.

In this situation, I didn't ask questions; I simply surrendered to Mrs. LaPlante's vision for me. Obviously, she saw something I didn't, so I didn't question it. Of course, I had no idea if I was good enough or even really what my role would be, but instead of worrying about it, I just kept showing up to practices and became the accompanist.

## MORE BREADCRUMBS

As is often the case, history repeats itself. This very same scenario played itself out for me at least three more times by the time I was in my freshman year of college.

During eleventh grade, my high school's drama department announced that it would be putting on a musical. This was my moment to shine! Finally, I would get the chance to sing and dance and act on stage! I was ready.

So I auditioned. I remember being one of the younger people there—it was mostly a senior cast, but that didn't stop me.

Eventually, the day came when the cast was announced. I was pulled aside by the directors, who told me, "Davide, we'd love you to be the musical director for the show—and we'd like you to sing two songs, too."

I was sold! I had no idea what being a musical director entailed, but it was the only offer on the table, and at that point in high school, I was looking for a lifeline. This was it.

Again, I didn't question their vision for me. I simply showed up and filled the role.

Two years later—in Canada at the time, high school was five (long) years—the drama teachers announced another musical. This time I was determined to sing, dance, and act on stage! I'll never forget approaching the drama teacher and show's director, Mr. Gorman, and declaring, "Sir, this year I want to *be in* the musical!"

Mr. Gorman stared back at me, and with an Irish twinkle in his eye, he replied, "Davide, we have a better idea. This year, you're going to write the musical!"

I didn't ask questions. I just showed up.

Over one week of spring break, Mr. Tos, the physics teacher, and I sat together to bring melodies and ideas to life for ten songs.

A few months later, I found myself a published Canadian composer.

## THE QUESTIONS YOU SHOULDN'T BE ASKING

Over the years, I've worked with thousands of performers, presenters, and speakers, and the one common thread that holds people back from becoming great is that they ask questions—the wrong questions. For example:

- Singer playing a main role in a musical: "How should I sing this line?"

- High school student preparing an in-class presentation: "What if I don't have five minutes' worth of material?"

- Successful entrepreneur, leader, and speaker preparing a TEDx talk: "What topic should I focus on, and what stories should I tell?"

Without fail, across every age, skill, and talent level, people ask the wrong questions that cause them to fall victim to comparanoia, wondering whether they are good enough, smart enough, talented enough, etc.

What are the right questions?

For a long time, I wasn't so sure myself, but here's what I've observed through my study and work in musical theater.

When I arrived at college, fresh off the success of my own musical score, I was definitely looking to continue my learning in the theater world. I didn't have to wait long. During the first week of classes, I attended my "Theater Production" elective, one of the few courses non-theater majors could take. (I was a music major.)

The instructor announced immediately that the course was being

# ASKING BETTER QUESTIONS

run in conjunction with the production so we would all take on roles in the production company. When he discovered I was a composer, he whisked me to an adjacent room with a grand piano and asked me to play some of what I had written.

After a few minutes, he interrupted and said, "Great! You are going to be the new musical director for the next four years for Vanier College Productions! I'm going to need you to write something that's maybe ninety-seconds long, multi-metric, maybe a little Streisand and a little *West Side Story*—we'll need it in a few weeks. See you next week in class!"

(Incidentally, "Wednesday and Thursday Sonia" from kindergarten was in the same class. I hadn't seen her since third grade!)

Without the opportunity even to ask any questions, I had to get to work. The first question I asked myself was, "Who can support me to bring this to life?" I was not a strong lyricist, and with such a short timeline, I knew I'd need to bring someone onboard. So I put out a call on the university messenger boards, and within days, I met my lyricist.

"Who do I need to be to get this done?" was the next question I asked.

I needed to be on a mission, efficient with my time, confident, and diligent in order to complete the task I had been given.

And I rose to the occasion.

I became the person I needed to become.

In my years as the musical director (and later as artistic director for a music series), I got to work very closely with the company's artistic director, Fred Thury, the same man who offered me the role of MD in my first week of classes. He became a mentor to me and is one of the people who shaped who I've become today.

One of the most vivid memories I have of Fred is of how he'd watch performers deliver lyrics. He'd sit there with his hands toward his face, fingers outstretched toward his mouth as if he were squeezing a stress ball in each hand, and he'd say, "Text, text, text…."

What I thought he meant was that he wanted singers and performers to enunciate more so the words would be clear.

What I came to learn in my own development as a musical director is that he was actually looking for the performer to show up through the words and the music.

As I grew into my own talents and instincts, I started to notice that the text and the performance itself were not enough. Especially during auditions, it became very clear to me that something was missing from most performers and performances. The note I would make for over 90 percent of auditionees was "I don't believe you" and "You don't believe you." In other words, the performer wasn't embodying the role or the lyrics.

Consider musical theater for a moment. Performers are required to bring abstract lyrics to life as they sing and, often, dance too. If you've ever read through lyrics, you'll know that they are usually non-linear, nearly nonsensical poetic structures that include a lot of repetition and rhyme. It's no wonder that I often didn't believe the performer.

But then, some performers could move audiences and create standing ovation moments. I became obsessed with these performers and performances, and it has been my life's work to discover the "X Factor," if you will, and learn how to recreate it so others can develop that skill and also deliver performances worthy of a standing ovation.

The breakthrough came when I heard the story of a famous music director who used to listen to his orchestra with his back turned to it. I decided I would adapt this idea to musical theater to see what I could learn and discover. What I discovered was pure magic, and it would radically change the way I approached direction and performance forever.

# ASKING BETTER QUESTIONS 51

In this chapter, I'm going to show you how you can use what I learned to take your speaking, singing, performing, and presenting of any kind to new heights that will move audiences into action, starting with a standing ovation.

My discovery was this: People don't hear or respond to what you're saying (or singing); they hear, feel, and respond to the way you're being.

It's so simple.

With my back turned, the only way to reach me was through honesty in performance. The performer had to believe what he or she was saying. He had to believe his motivations. She had to become the character infused with all the emotion, history, desires, and wants that would bring the lyrics and music to life. Nearly none of that was found in the script and music.

## THE BIG QUESTION

An exploration of questions would be incomplete without a mention of the big question: Why?

With his Why Movement, Simon Sinek has catalyzed thousands upon thousands who are operating more in alignment with their purpose. He has encouraged leaders around the globe to be on-purpose and to uncover their purposes.

In my own experiences with thousands of performers, presenters, and speakers, the issue comes when the individual or group (in the case of a full cast, or even a company) doesn't know his, her, or its why.

Asking the question "Why?" often translates to "What's my purpose?" That's a forward-thinking question, rather than one that honors and celebrates the breadcrumbs of your identity that you've dropped your entire life.

Even in the performance realm, "Why?" can translate to the age-old question, "What's my motivation?" This question is commonly asked by method actors who rely on intent and purpose to inform their performances.

"Why?" can be a difficult question to answer. In 2011, as I stood watching my house burn down (I'll tell that story in Chapter 12), and for many months (probably even years) into the aftermath, the only answer I could come up with to why I did anything in this life (the purpose of any of it) was that there was absolutely no purpose to anything.

I've literally crisscrossed the globe in search of the meaning of life, and finally, I've realized that asking "Why?" often derails our true purpose because it causes us to look externally for something that is not found "out there."

Purpose is intrinsic. It is a part of you, just like your genetic code. It's in your DNA.

It's *who* you are.

Eureka!

## THE QUESTION YOU SHOULD BE ASKING

Instead of asking and looking for "Why?", start asking "Whom do I need to be?"

As a speaker, whom do you need to be to transform your audience? To shift its thinking? To gift it with a new perspective?

As a leader, whom do you need to be to lead your people to their own success? To lead a movement? To inspire other leaders?

As a visionary, whom do you need to be to attract and lead your tribe to greatness?

Consider asking yourself, "Who am I?" and "Who have I always been?" to reveal your essence as will be shown in your *Everyday Extraordinary Storytelling Book*.

In my own early work, I had a model that I referred to as "Why to How to Wow!" It addressed the most common mistake speakers and leaders make: asking what and how before they understand why they are even in action at all. My process would take you through a series of questions starting with why, followed by who, what, and finally, how.

I've adjusted that model in more recent years to, "Who to How to Wow!" (Wow, of course, is the standing ovation moment.) The first questions to consider are: Who am I? Who have I been? Who do I want to be? Who is my audience right now? Who do I want my audience to be?

The question of who directly informs why you do what you do and why you are who you are (whole and complete, right now).

## ON PURPOSE

You arrived with purpose, and while you may find purpose in service of others, the specifics of what your purpose truly is are already inside of you waiting for you to (re)discover (or maybe remember) them.

As yogi, leader, and visionary Baron Baptiste teaches, instead of constantly looking to fix yourself, or finding the next thing to move on to, what if you actually took time to become yourself? How much more authentic and real would you show up? How might you move others into action if you were operating from your own miracle rather than trying to fill someone else's expectation for who you should be?

Take a look at your *Everyday Extraordinary Storytelling Book*. Review each incident and ask yourself these two questions for each:

1. How did I react/respond in this situation?
2. Who was I being?

Notice the pattern that emerges.

Based on the answers to the above, who have you been throughout your life? It might not all be positive or what you want or expect, but getting to know who you've been throughout your life will allow you to uncover who you truly are.

For example, when I look back on my life, I could say: I am a leader. I am loved. I am creative. I am (sometimes) afraid. I am overly apologetic.

I am _____  I am _____

I am _____  I am _____

I am _____  I am _____

I am _____  I am _____

# SPOTLIGHT: UNAPOLOGETIC INFLUENCER

## UNCHAINED
**BY CARSON COOPER**

*Carson Cooper is a coach, speaker, and mediator. You can learn more about him at CarsonCooper.com.*

To live unchained is to live with authenticity, courage, and vulnerability. Being unchained is living with passion, with purpose, and at your true potential. It means seeking out discomfort, overcoming boredom and frustration, and finding out what you are truly made of.

For me, being unchained means that everyone is a leader by choice or default. I choose to live my life as an open, daring, trusting leader. Being a leader means having the willingness to fight with your parents to move out with your first love; to quit your full-time secure job to be an entrepreneur; to let go of a toxic relationship; to love fiercely despite being hurt; and to stand in front of a room of people who hate you and say you want to hear, understand, and walk with them. It means moving back in with your parents to repair the relationship and save money for a huge life goal. It means cancelling a night out with friends to meditate, journal, cook dinner, and spend time with yourself. It means being generous, empathetic, and in service even when you feel like you can't be. Ultimately, being unchained is being in integrity even when it's inconvenient.

Let me take you on a journey where being unchained is the destination with an unlikely path. In January 2018, I was at the base camp at Mt. Kilimanjaro. The guide pointed to where the peak was. I looked off into the dark, thinking, *What did I get myself into?*

My guide briefed us on what we were about to undertake: "It's six hours, three miles, a 5,000-foot elevation gain, and -32 degrees. Don't ask how far we have gone; don't ask how far we have to go; stay together, and take one step at a time."

It was 11 p.m. We had been hiking for five days to get to the base camp. The guide had explained that Mt. Kilimanjaro was so steep that if you were to see where you were going, mentally, it would be too tough to complete. It was hiked at night so you couldn't see where you were going and could only take one step at a time.

To explain how I had gotten to this point, let's rewind to one year prior, January 2017, when I had the following conversation with a coach.

Coach: What is your biggest dream?

Me: To take people around the world on backpack trips and coach them.

Coach: Where would you take them?

Me: Mt. Kilimanjaro.

Coach: How long have you wanted it?

Me: Since I was eight.

Coach: When do you want to do it?

Me: Oh, in five to ten years.

Coach: (taken aback) No, when do you really want to do it...?

Me: Well, I guess, one year from now.

In January of 2017, I publicly declared to a room of strangers that in January of 2018, I was going to hike Mt. Kilimanjaro, not knowing how it was going to happen or even if it was possible. You see, in January 2017, I had a full-time job I loved, yet something felt off. I couldn't imagine taking three weeks off, let alone having vacation time. I was more than $30,000 in debt, and in the worst shape of my life.

This trip made me think about life, relationships, love, entrepreneurship, goals, and dreams. If I had known the effort it was going to take to get there, would I have chosen to make the journey in the first place?

I would love to say it was easy, that I was strong, confident, and courageous the entire time. In reality, while getting there, I endured a failed business partnership and health issues. On the mountain, three different times, I burst into tears, wanting to stop, not knowing if I could make it, and on the verge of giving up. The difficult journey reminded me of coming out, my first heartbreak, losing my first job to near bankruptcy and a lawsuit, medical issues with my parents, academic probation in college, and starting my own business and making no income for two years.

As I look back on my treck up Mt. Kilimanjaro and the different parts of my life, every single step was worth it; every single step made me who I am. Every single step released the chains just a little bit more.

By the time I left one year later in January of 2018, I had a job doing what I loved wholeheartedly, and it was no issue taking time off. I paid for the entire trip in cash, and I was still in the worst shape of my life!

Look at your hands...

What story do your hands tell you?

What life journey do they show you?

What are you noticing?

Are you living your life unchained?

Ladies and gentlemen, too many people don't start from fear of failing. Yet if you don't start, you will never know what you are capable of.

Tons of peaks may exist on the way to your summit. You may be at base camp and unable to see where you are going. Trust that you have everything you need inside of you. You deserve to let it out and live unchained.

Own your mindset, own your impact. Let yourself stumble and take one step at a time.

Let me share one more personal story with you that illustrates what it means to be unchained.

I was at a toy drive fundraiser when I started talking about my work.

A person there instantly spat at me in disgust, "Where are we at—a staff meeting?"

For a split-second, I was angry. In the next second, I laughed. Then for another second, I was embarrassed.

After the event, I had the following thoughts:

- I am not interesting enough.
- I am not good enough.
- I can't talk about anything else but work.
- No one understands me or cares.

Fast forward to another event I attended where everyone was there to ignite their lives and were turning their dreams into reality, together. We all talked for three days straight, ten hours each day about our jobs, about work...no wait, about our purpose!

It was so incredible to be around a tribe of people who were inspired and reaching for a life filled with joy, freedom, and passion.

What I learned from that experience was:

- My job is my purpose! I love talking about what I do. It's part of my being. It doesn't feel like work at all.

- Never again will I allow my negative beliefs to get me down or let me think I am "not good enough," "not interesting enough," or that I can't share what I am passionate about.

- No longer will I take on others' beliefs that I cannot do what I love for a living.

- No longer will I choose to believe I cannot make money doing what I am passionate about.

This weekend, a speaker at Life On Fire's Ignite event shared a quote:

> "Don't change your act; change your audience."
>
> — Eddie Garson

This quote confirmed for me that despite other people's beliefs at the fundraiser, I am on purpose!

My vision is for all people to see themselves as leaders!

I am committed to building a tribe where we are comfortable talking about our purpose and what we *love* all the time. I am committed to building a tribe where we celebrate each other, support each other, and love on each other! I hope you will join me in this worthy endeavor.

**UN** ARE YOU READY TO BE
UNATTACHED?

# ACCEPTING YOURSELF

"It turns out that failure is the best tool we have—it's the only way we really learn."

— Eric Whitacre

Now that you've begun to ask yourself the question that will begin to uncover and lead you to your personal greatness, you can start to sort through the data of your life (who you've been throughout) and determine the truth of who you are.

Sometimes (in fact, most often), you won't love what you discover when you review who you've been at different points in your life.

Now what? How do you reconcile who you've been with who you want to be, and who you believe yourself to be? How do you actually become that person—the one you know in your heart of hearts is ready to thrive, to speak, and to lead others to success?

It's one thing to say, "Just accept yourself, and move on." It's a whole other thing to implement that thinking.

Some of us (myself included) learn the hard way. The good news is that I've come out on the other side and am on a mission to share what I've learned through my own experiences, research, and observation.

In 2009, I turned thirty-three. Apparently, big things happen at thirty-three. For me, growing up Catholic, it meant that I was now the "age of Christ" when his story came to an end. While I would joke lightly about it, nothing could have prepared me for the revelation I would receive that summer.

I was in my third year as the head of a high school music department, and fresh off a near hit after pitching a major television station for a children's multi-platform educational series. (Near hit, or near miss, we didn't get the green light.)

I was feeling defeated. I was feeling that my time as a teacher was limited. It's not that I didn't love my students; it's just that I felt limited by the system.

When I looked back on my own life and who I'd been, I saw so many instances of me being an achiever, a doer, a winner.

By that point, I had already traveled extensively, been valedictorian (twice), received honors and aced multiple degree and diploma programs, been featured in the newspaper, and landed multiple jobs in first interviews...so, in retrospect, the "No" from the television network was hard to take.

I can safely say that at thirty-three, I was experiencing a life crisis.

I know you can relate. High achievers do so much, yet we rarely stop to celebrate anything for long.

Take a moment to celebrate your accolades and achievements. Acknowledge the things that seem *regular* to you but are, in fact, extraordinary to non-high achievers. Take time now to write them all down:

_____

_____

_____

# ACCEPTING YOURSELF

_____

_____

_____

_____

_____

_____

## DISTRACTIONS

Your life screams out at you through everything you've achieved, but because we are so unfamiliar with being ourselves, life presents distractions. Actually, we look for and create them.

In early 2009, I was commissioned by the Yellowknife Choral Society to arrange a piece for an upcoming concert. When I finished the piece, I traveled to Yellowknife (in the Canadian Arctic) to work with the choir.

I was stung.

The week in a new setting really gave me a fresh perspective on life and what was possible.

Let me take a moment to share that I absolutely hate the cold! The average daily temperature in town was -40 F degrees. I even spent a few days in the High Arctic where the daytime temperature was below -90!

So, the fact that I fell in love with the Arctic speaks volumes about just how serious my impending distraction (crisis) was.

When I returned to Toronto from this short trip, I was a man obsessed. Every thought was on starting over in the new city I had fallen in love with. There was also an opportunity to write more for the choral society, and the local high school (the only one) was soon to be interviewing for a new music teacher! Everything was in perfect alignment.

I packed all my belongings and prepared my home to be rented out for a year. On July 1, Canada Day, my best friend Martha drove me to the airport. I'll never forget the words she said to me that day as we left my home. "Davide, you know, you don't have to do this…. You should just talk to your parents."

Nothing could have convinced me to change my decision at that point.

The first three days in Yellowknife were amazing. I felt free and light.

On day four, everything changed. I likened it to the rush of going on a third date, after the first two have been spectacular, and all of a sudden, it's like someone has put on the *reality glasses* and you have the proverbial "I think I've made a mistake" moment.

I felt like a fool. And yet, I journeyed on. I had made my choice, and I was going to make it right, even in the face of things going from bad to worse. (Entrepreneurship 101, right?)

I was, for all intents and purposes, homeless. I would house-sit for absentee homeowners I'd find on the local grocery store's announcement board.

That's when I met Toby the Pomeranian. He was left in my care for ten days. I can still vividly remember Toby's owners telling me about their special little man and his ulcer (which would nearly give *me* an ulcer).

We *did not* get along. Day after day, Toby played tricks on me, locked me out, and even bit me!

Finally, I decided to have a *come to Jesus* talk with my canine nemesis. "Toby, this can't continue; something's got to change! Tomorrow, I'm going to wake up and love you like you've never been loved!"

The next morning, I greeted Toby with a big smile. I continued to speak and demonstrate kindness and love all day long, no matter what.

# ACCEPTING YOURSELF

Toby responded with love. By 3:30 p.m., he was curled up in my lap with my own dog, Galileo. Toby was even giving me doggy kisses.

In that moment, I learned one of my biggest life lessons to date. It hit me like an Arctic iceberg!

*I* was the problem! It wasn't that Toby was spoiled or had a bad attitude. It was actually me. As I started to take a look at my life, I came to realize that the problem in my entire life was me!

For a moment, I felt defeated. Only for a moment, because just as soon as I realized I was the problem, I realized I could also be the solution! And I celebrated!

The bigger realization that hit me like a second, very hard and cold iceberg, was that the actual problem was that I didn't like, love, or accept myself....

Wow, that one really hurt, and because it did, I knew it to be absolutely true. I had lived my entire life until this point denying my true identity. Especially for the last thirteen years, I had known without a doubt that I was gay, and yet, I had never embraced it for myself. I never truly admitted it to myself, and I never felt it was okay.

As a result, I kept everyone at a distance. My relationships with absolutely everyone in my life, from family and friends to even the people I had dated, was detached, distant, and mostly non-existent.

What could become possible for me if I changed my relationship with myself first—if I truly accepted who I was?

Was it possible that in accepting myself, I would also be able to nurture better relationships?

Could I positively impact those around me just like I had, in under a day, positively impacted Toby and the way he related to me?

I had the proof, and the results astounded me and lifted me out of my depression.

Over the next several weeks, I continued the process of deeper acceptance of myself. Multiple times throughout the day, I would look into the mirror and introduce myself to the new me. I would stare into my eyes and repeat over and over, "Davide, I appreciate you! I thank you! I love you! You are a miracle!"

And so my journey to the Arctic was actually a journey of acceptance. By removing myself from my regular environment with no real Plan B, I exposed my weaknesses.

I don't suggest you up and move your life to determine whether or not you accept yourself. However, I encourage you to consider with brutal objectivity the level to which you accept yourself—all of you—because I've learned that self-acceptance plays a major factor in how the rest of the world (even your pets!) sees and interacts with you.

Be honest with yourself; what aspects of you do you not fully accept? It could be something physical, it could be some aspect of your temperament, or it could even be some of your habits. List those things below:

_____

_____

_____

_____

_____

_____

For each of the things you listed above, write a statement of acceptance and positive reinforcement that you will recite every morning and every evening in the mirror.

## ACCEPTING YOURSELF

_____

_____

_____

_____

What will become possible for you when you fully accept and celebrate all of who you are?

_____

_____

_____

_____

_____

What are you celebrating right now?

_____

_____

_____

_____

_____

# SPOTLIGHT:
# UNAPOLOGETIC INFLUENCER

## UNLOVED
### BY RE PEREZ

*Re Perez is a brand consultant, keynote speaker, and the founder and CEO of BRANDING FOR THE PEOPLE. You can learn more about him at BrandingForThePeople.com.*

One online definition of unloved is "not loved or cared for: feeling neglected and unloved." That said, the real insight comes from the word love and one's relationship to love. Love refers to having a warm feeling of affection or deep affection. Typically, one's relationship to love relates to the love you receive from someone else (in other words, it's an external thing). Personally, I take a more spiritual approach to it. To me, love is a state of being in which a person feels nurtured, fulfilled, and full of integrity. And, to be clear, that state of being can come from within and is not reliant on another person. Love has nothing to do with sex or even intimacy.

Therefore, feeling unloved is a state of being in which one does not feel nurtured, fulfilled, or filled with integrity.

When I was born, an inaccurate rumor was spread that my mother had cheated on my dad, and I was the resulting product. So for a long time, my father did not believe I was his son. Subconsciously, this situation registered for me as "I am unloved by my own dad." Love was questioned. Therefore, I did not feel nurtured, fulfilled, or filled with integrity in one of my most important early relationships. Growing up, this feeling of being unloved directly correlated with my relationship with my father. However, as I've done personal development and inner work, I've learned that love comes from within (self-love), and it's more powerful when you can generate your own sense of love rather than relying on someone's else's love.

Being unapologetic in the context of being unloved means I am not afraid (nor do I care) if someone does not *love* me. On a granular level, I don't really care if someone doesn't like me. It's not that I wish to be hated or not liked—it's that seeking someone else's love is not my context in life. It's not my context for my business or personal relationships.

If anything, whenever someone does not love me—or I have a feeling of being unloved by a person—it really becomes a motivator for me to excel even further. I then show that my own self-love, drive, character, wisdom, and talents will supersede someone else's lack of love for me. So, being unapologetic about being unloved is a driving force for me to become the best person I can possibly be.

From what I've just said, you could probably extrapolate that if you ever feel unloved, that's on you. You have control over whether or not you love or don't love yourself, whether or not you care about or nurture yourself, and whether or not you are in harmony with your own personal life purpose or mission.

If you do feel unloved, how can you resolve the situation? First, identify all your reasons and belief systems and the conversations you're having with yourself as to why you don't love yourself. Transform that conversation into a very simple statement: I am love.

Repeat this process every time you find yourself feeling unloved. Repeat it as often as need be. Come to believe it and soon you will notice a change in both yourself and in how others respond to you. When you come to love yourself, you will discover that anything is possible.

**UN** ARE YOU READY TO BE
UNAFRAID?

# ACTING COURAGEOUSLY

> "Until you're ready to look foolish, you'll never have the possibility of being great."
>
> — Cher

The journey to unconditional self-acceptance (good, bad, or ugly) causes so many people to live locked and frozen, waiting just off to the side—in the wings of life's grand stage.

Perhaps the most painful part, as I discovered myself, is that we are so often the problem. In my Arctic experience, I realized that I had a choice, and despite having to give up my need to be right in order to have my freedom, I think you would agree that freedom outweighs righteousness in every scenario.

Now that you have made the choice to experience your personal freedom by accepting all of yourself, you can begin to chip away at the thoughts and beliefs that have ruled your life and kept you small. Some people would have you believe that tackling life, whether it be business, love, public speaking, or leading a multinational company, requires great courage. I've found, however, that simply choosing courage is not a foolproof path to success.

In my own transformational work, I have come to discover that true greatness and success (and freedom) require what most people would consider the polar opposite of courage: vulnerability.

What if acting courageously actually required you to be vulnerable first, before and in the process of "being courageous"?

Can acting courageously without being vulnerable actually have negative effects?

## RUNNING AWAY FROM YOURSELF

I was bullied as a child, a teen, and even as an adult.

You know how, as kids, we sometimes get great ideas that we are absolutely convinced will solve all our problems? I had a major Eureka moment in the eighth grade that I was positive would radically alter the course of my life.

At Our Lady of Victory, when you got to the eighth grade, you had a big decision to make. I'll never forget the day Mrs. Tucker handed out the catalogues from which we'd choose which high school to apply to. We had waited for this day with great anticipation, and it was finally here!

For me, this was an opportunity to break free from my bullies and all the history that had plagued my ten years of grade school. Faggot, fairy, queer, gaylord, pussy—those were just a few of the names I'd heard daily, and often multiple times per day. It was rough, but I knew it would all be behind me soon.

While most students were encouraged to choose the school within the district (choose = forced because the truth was schoolboards didn't really want to allow students to move outside their districts), I had *one* choice—a school I'd have to take a subway *and* a bus to get to. It was a school I had visited during one of the science fairs I had participated in. (I was quite the over-achiever when it came to the science fair, but that's a story for another time.)

Bishop Francis Marrocco/Thomas Merton Catholic Secondary School (affectionately known as "M and M") was huge! It was a four-floor facility that included two gymnasiums, a greenhouse, a courtyard, a beautiful theater space, two large music rooms, and even a swimming pool.

The best part: Only seven of my closest friends were applying to get in, which meant I'd leave all my bullies behind.

It turned out that getting accepted to this school was quite the process, and frankly, I'm not sure I or any of my friends were ever accepted officially. When we arrived on day one, none of us were on any of the attendance records. Same on day two, three, five, and ten.... It took well over two weeks before our names finally showed up. I think the school's administration finally just realized we weren't going to leave and added us to the records.

I had a great first month of school. I even jumped at the opportunity to go on a field trip when my English teacher announced there were a few spots open to travel to Stratford, Ontario, to see a Shakespeare play. The trip was for seniors (Grade 13 back then), but I didn't let that stop me.

Shortly after returning from the field trip, I remember being at my locker when a couple of students walked by and one said to the other, "Is that the faggot you were telling me about?"

If I could fit inside my locker, I would have crawled in, by choice, and stayed there.

Over the next few weeks, it became clear to me that my act of courage to move to a new school without any friends had not solved my problems.

I was crushed, heartbroken, and quite confused. None of these kids knew me, so how did they know my secret that I had left behind in grade school?

Things went from bad to worse. I guess I couldn't blame some of my grade school friends for not wanting to be associated with me. Being a teenager is hard enough without being the target of bullying.

However, I was definitely not prepared when one friend encouraged some bullies I had attracted on the public bus.

Almost every day, on the way home, a group of boys on the bus would pick on me. Even my one female friend would side with them because she fancied one of the boys. From the back of the bus, she would yell to me, "What's wrong, Davide? Are you scared?"

Scared? I was horrified, convinced that these guys were going to beat me up or worse. I even started getting off at different stops so they wouldn't find out where I lived.

What did I do about it? I tried to act courageously. I was given the advice from my other friends to "ignore" them and just be confident. However, I can assure you that this tactic doesn't work. Day after day, my confidence eroded and diminished. Soon, I started to feel very lonely and dark thoughts began to rule me.

For over two years, I suffered in the wake of acting courageously. I simply didn't know what else to do.

## LIFE WILL THROW YOU A LIFELINE

Fortunately, the high school musical came along during eleventh grade. My participation in this quintessential high school experience would save my life—literally.

Some may think that to be in a high school musical, especially as a boy, you need to have courage. I beg to differ. The courage, in fact, comes from being willing to share yourself openly. As Cher said, you have to be willing to "look foolish."

Since nothing else I was doing was making me happy (or popular), I surrendered to the process and the directors. Playing the split role of musical director and performer was definitely challenging, but so much fun! With each rehearsal, my confidence grew, until costume day arrived.

The directors' vision for my character was a musical director with a bit of an off-the-wall personality as a manic artist, who just happened to forget to put on his pants.

No big deal. I was positioned upstage left in a corner, seated behind my piano—except for the scene where I had to climb the scaffolding to deliver a line. Yes, I would be seen without any pants on in front of the entire student body and community.

I'm not exactly sure what possessed me, but I figured if I was going to do this, I'd go all in (a topic I'll explore further in an upcoming chapter), so I found the glitziest pair of boxers I could. They were black satin with holographic hearts on them. I found a matching bow tie to match!

Vulnerable was an understatement! And I did it, and the results were, to me, shocking.

This was the first real situation in high school where I actually showed up as myself, and the audiences loved it!

Perhaps I was on to something. I started becoming more vulnerable in classes and while I was out and about in school. I became more daring during drama classes. I remember one performance where my group, led by a friend who fancied himself an acclaimed impresario and visionary of thespian arts (ahem), said I would commit social suicide if I went through with my idea to wear a garbage bag during a short play we had put together. He especially warned me against tearing off the bag during the final scene where my dialogue was all about cutting through the noise and peeling back the layers.... However, it made perfect sense to me.

My friend was so horrified that on performance day, he acted neither courageously nor vulnerably; instead, he stayed home. I, on the other hand, showed up in the trash bag, and at the end of the sketch, I slowly ripped it off. I'll never forget thinking that this moment would either make or break me. I remember staring directly into the eyes of the hundred or so students who packed the room to watch. I was determined, performing from my vision.

Well, it worked. I became even more respected for the vulnerability I displayed on stage *and* the courage I had to execute my vision so creatively.

## VULNERABLE COURAGE

Vulnerability has served me well through life. In fact, only in the times when I've abandoned it have I found myself miserable.

Take the "Arctic Expedition." Leading up to that transition, I was simply going through the motions (without emotion). I convinced myself to act courageously, no matter what. I didn't really talk to anyone about it or share how I really felt—that I was lost, unsure of my career, lonely even. Not even in those final moments before leaving did I share openly with my best friend, despite her trying to open the door to the conversation I needed to have.

You see, Martha had known me my entire life, and to this day, she's my longest and closest friend.

The words she spoke to me before she took me to the airport, "Davide, you know, you don't have to do this.... You should just talk to your parents" would ultimately haunt me in Yellowknife.

What she was talking about was the fact that, at thirty-three, I hadn't come out to my parents yet.

It was one of those things. Most of us have *something* we don't share with our parents. For me, this was the big (gigantic) elephant in the room. Although I didn't know it at the time, Martha's intuition was spot on.

When I had my big aha moment that I was the problem *and* the solution to everything in my life, almost immediately, I began to move into action to become the solution. One way I did that was to be incredibly vulnerable, with *everyone*.

I started calling up my friends to come out to them—probably as practice because I knew I'd need to get comfortable with it before telling my parents.

One by one, I would call or Facebook message someone close to me and tell them.

Without fail, nearly every single person's response was, "Davide, I know...."

Side note: Of course, I knew you knew, but I had finally mustered the courage to share it. If you're ever in the situation where someone you love comes out to you and you've already known, do them (and me) a favor and just say "I love you." Trust me, the last thing I needed as I was ripping off the Band-Aids of vulnerability was to discover I was the last person who realized I was gay.

In any case, here, once again, vulnerability served me and provided me with so many blessings. And the beauty is this: Being vulnerable *is* an act of great courage. It is, by far, the most transformational experience I've ever been through. To this day, the moments when I am open and vulnerable are the ones that provide the biggest revelations and transformations.

## VULNERABILITY IS A GROWTH ZONE

Your growing edge lives in your ability to be vulnerable. While some may argue great leaders do not show weaknesses, I argue that they do show their humanity. Sometimes that humanity shows through in the stories they share or in the moments when they poke fun at themselves. It doesn't always have to be a grand gesture.

Being vulnerable opens you up to receiving. Are you ready and willing to receive?

In what area of your life can you be more vulnerable or show more vulnerability?

_____

_____

_____

With whom can you be more vulnerable?

_____

_____

_____

How will you be more vulnerable?

_____

_____

_____

What do you see becoming possible as a direct result of you being more vulnerable?

_____

_____

_____

By what date will you practice this vulnerability?

_____

_____

# SPOTLIGHT: UNAPOLOGETIC INFLUENCER

## UNAFRAID
**BY NIRAJ MENDIS**

*Niraj Mendis is a speaker, author, and coach. You can learn more about him at NirajMendis.com.*

For me, being unafraid means operating from a space of self-love and taking massive action regardless of what others think about your decisions. It means continuously moving forward without any fear or anxiety, knowing the universe is there to support your decisions. It also means understanding that any obstacle or sense of fear that arises is an opportunity to learn, grow, and expand.

I grew up during a civil war in Sri Lanka, but I never suspected my fear and anxiety were not the result of that external war; rather, it was an internal civil war I was fighting. We are all in a state of civil war with our inner critic, that voice that says, "You can't do it. You're not good enough. You are a loser."

Being unapologetic means silencing your inner critic, loving yourself unconditionally, and leading a transparent life. Today, I am unafraid to speak my truth or inspire others to show up authentically so they can build heart-to-heart connections and live in a peaceful world.

Being afraid is an artificial construct we have created. It has an imaginary box around it. The box's walls act as bumper rails that hold us back from following our dreams and living purposeful lives.

Once you break out from the shackles of fear, you realize you have an infinite amount of potential. When you focus on what you really want to accomplish, the support and resources will show up.

To learn how to live unafraid, first be the better person and have an authentic conversation with your inner critic to resolve the internal civil war. You'll notice that once you have peace inside you, your environment will become peaceful and you'll live a balanced life.

Being unafraid means living in self-love. For years, I hated myself to the point where I would self-sabotage myself and wasn't able to achieve my full potential. Loving yourself and living in your truth will allow you to have the confidence and positive mindset needed to fuel your desires, visions, and dreams.

Part of how I learned to be unafraid was by attending a training in which all the participants were asked to bungee jump off a cliff. Leading up to that jump, we had done many exercises to build up our confidence and practice making decisions in a decisive way. As I walked onto the ramp thousands of feet above the ground, the wind was blowing into my face, but I was not afraid to jump. I knew any fear running through my head would be imaginary because I had faith in that moment that the universe supported me in my decision to jump. All the exercises we did up to that point had been preparation for this moment. I just had to have faith that the cord would support me and that the people handling me were trained to do their jobs. As I jumped, a sense of peace came over me, and quickly thereafter, adrenaline poured through my veins. It was an indescribable moment.

This opportunity to be unafraid did not come easily to me. I had been afraid most of my life. Only in the last decade have I been able to overcome the fear of war and what others would think of me if I followed my heart.

The turning point for me was my thirtieth birthday. By then, I had done all the things that family, culture, and society had said to do to achieve happiness: get a degree, find a good job, buy a house, have a relationship, and so on. However, I still wasn't satisfied with my life. Self-love was lacking, and I was drinking, smoking, and overworking myself while trying to climb the corporate ladder. Through yoga and meditation, I was able to get in touch with myself and detoxify my body and mind. Self-love and treating my body and mind as a temple shifted me to become unafraid.

That shift has allowed me to vibrate at a different level and to attract whatever I desire into my life. I am able to manifest things I wasn't able to do before. When you know your intentions are clear and you feel no ill against anybody else, then you can manifest anything you desire.

While living in fear, you might be able to get by; however, you will not be able to live out your highest potential because self-love is the full expression of unafraid. Without self-love, you cannot love another, and fear is an artificial construct created based on certain situations and circumstances.

If I were still afraid today, I would still be self-sabotaging myself, and I would be unable to love others the way I love them now. I would be playing small and I wouldn't have achieved financial success or realized inner peace.

A better world awaits all of us when we choose to live unafraid. I invite you to take the leap. The world will catch you, I promise.

**UN** ARE YOU READY TO BE
UNBURDENED?

# LETTING GO

"What's the greater risk? Letting go of what people think—or letting go of how I feel, what I believe, and who I am?"

— Brené Brown

You've identified incidents in your life that have caused you pain and discomfort. Through the *Everyday Extraordinary Storytelling Book*, I've encouraged you to unearth these incidents and who you truly are. By taking a look at who you are and resolving to accept yourself today as a miracle (whole, complete, and confident), you can start to crack the layers of life that have asked you to be and act in a way that ignores your natural emotional compass.

In the last chapter, I invited you to get vulnerable with yourself and those around you. In my own experience and observation, vulnerability is the most courageous human act.

In exposing vulnerability, you will also discover incidents and life history that will challenge you. The challenge will be not to harden your shell, or close yourself off, and instead, to act with courage. You know now, however, that true courage doesn't include ignoring reality (which requires vulnerability).

In this chapter, I invite you to explore aspects of your life and history that challenge you. What will it take for you to *let go* of the past so you can live fully in the present and, in turn, fully in your purpose (which is *only* possible in the present).

I've identified three major areas in which you can practice and exercise the "letting go" muscle:

1. **Business or external factors:** These provide the risk of becoming internal, so you need to *let go* before they do.
2. **Family:** Comes with its own challenges and definitely requires special attention to build the *muscle memory* that will support your learning of *letting go*.
3. **Beliefs or internal factors:** Definitely the most complex and hardest to *let go*.

Let's look at how you can practice letting go in each area.

## LETTING GO IN BUSINESS

Everyday life, and especially business, creates situations, incidents, and scenarios that challenge you. They are external challenges that often end up being fully internalized, thus ruining your day, and in some cases, threatening to ruin your life.

In 2010, I thought it would be a great idea to get into the yoga studio business. It was not. Despite the thousands of red flags throughout the process, I am a man of my word, so when I declare something, I go with it—all the way to the end. In this case, the end almost became my end.

To give you the condensed *Reader's Digest* version, I had fallen in love with the practice of yoga, and the studio where I practiced was looking to open its first franchise location. I love being a trailblazer, so I didn't waste any time expressing my interest in going after the opportunity.

# LETTING GO

At about the same time, my friend and business partner in my successful theater production company venture had a baby—her first. Upon the baby's arrival, I visited her and shared my desire to get into the yoga business. She was literally breast-feeding her baby during this conversation.

Some moments in life are unexplainable. This became one of them. Without skipping a beat, and while sitting on the couch, baby wrapped and feeding, she said, "I'm in!"

Because we had a long history together, I didn't even question that she didn't necessarily have the finances, she didn't have the same love for the specific kind of yoga the studio would teach, or that she was a new mom. None of those thoughts deterred me.

By September 2010, the studio was a reality. We had chosen a beautiful red brick building with fourteen-foot ceilings and wall-to-wall windows. We had outfitted it with Canadian Maple floors, heated ceiling panels, showers, a couple of offices (so we could also run our theater business and rent out space to massage therapists and wellness practitioners), and even a custom reception desk made from reclaimed barn board. Did I mention the studio was in downtown Toronto? In other words, it was a very expensive venture. The rent on the space alone was $10,000 per month.

It didn't take long to discover that covering the monthly lease would take a lot of yoga classes! At the same time, I happened to talk to some other yoga studio owners who were celebrating that, now in their third year of operations, and after investing $3,000,000, they were finally breaking even. (Insert myocardial infarction here.)

To make matters worse, we opened our studio during the height of what I like to call the Age of Groupon, and we signed up, with bells on. In other words, we had sold over one thousand vouchers that offered purchasers twenty-one classes for $20 (two deals per person).

It was certainly a successful campaign. But for who?

After the deal went into effect, a typical studio front-desk interaction went something like this:

Me: Welcome! Great to see you back!

Yogi: Hi, I just used my last class on my pass last session. Will you be having another deal soon?

Me: We have loved seeing you at the studio so much. That was our one time "Welcome to the studio" deal. We do have packages that fit any budget, from single classes to packs, monthly and yearly memberships.

Yogi: Ah...yeah, that's okay. The studio down the street has a deal going on right now. I'll consider coming back when you have the next deal.

Me: [No words]

I was blown away that people actually thought a studio could run on seventeen-cents-per-class yoga. In actuality, we figured we were definitely losing money with every single class we ran that was filled with deal holders.

It was a tough lesson to take.

As you can imagine, things went from bad to worse. By February 2011, I had stopped eating. (I couldn't afford it.) By May, I was essentially bankrupt and my partner in the studio kindly invited me not to come back because she would find another partner more committed to the project. By September, the studio went bankrupt.

I'm not sharing this story to air the details, point the finger, make myself right, or make anyone else wrong. I've painted the picture for you so you can see that a lot of resentment (from many parties) was created by this situation.

When I finally declared the business bankrupt, having lost well over $100,000 of my own savings, dug myself into major debt, lost investors' money, lost my friendship with my longtime business partner, lost my confidence, and nearly lost my life, it was not easy just to *let go*.

I was angry.

I was righteous.

I was hurt.

There were things my business partner had and hadn't done that hurt me.... Things that the franchisers had and hadn't done.... It was truly a laundry list of things where I could play victim, but I knew that would never afford me my freedom.

The situation was pure hell.

In the end, it all came down to me making a choice. I could choose to be right, angry, hurt, and a perpetual victim, or I could choose freedom (which would not be available to me if I chose the former because I would forever carry all the negative feelings with me).

So I chose freedom. It wasn't simple. I constantly (hourly) had to remind myself that I was choosing freedom over the past hurt, mistakes, things that had been *done to me*, or whatever I had created in my mind. And even for the things where I was absolutely positive I was *right*, I let go of my need to be right over my desire to live free of the stress and weight of the past.

Where in your business life can you choose freedom over being right?

_____

_____

_____

_____

_____

By choosing freedom, what will become possible for you?

_____

_____

_____

What can you celebrate right now? (An aha, a realization, or simply a current reality?)

_____

_____

_____

## LETTING GO WITH FAMILY

While family is essentially an external force, letting go of family drama is most definitely an intermediate to advanced practice, which is why I've given it its own section.

I suppose you could say that when it comes to family, mine came with a lot of cultural and historical strings.

My Italian immigrant parents brought with them to Canada many *old world* ideas and expectations of what their two sons should and shouldn't be or do.

Earlier, I shared that the delivery room nurse was overjoyed to announce that she felt I had the hands of a pianist. Nothing could have perplexed my parents more. In their minds, three options were available: doctor, lawyer, and accountant.

My older brother followed the path toward being an accountant. My parents deduced I wasn't smart enough (or they were afraid to commit me or themselves to the amount of schooling required) to be a doctor, so my destiny (according to them) was to become a lawyer.

You can imagine their horror when I came home during my senior year and announced that I was going to pursue music. I'm pretty sure my father went to break something, and my mother started praying heavily under her breath. (Oh, yes, I grew up Catholic.)

What about when I decided to take a detour into the travel industry? I worked for Club Med, hotels, resorts, at the airport, as a travel agent, and I even became a flight attendant.

I was so terrified to tell my parents that I had been accepted for flight attendant training that I decided not to tell them. Instead, I told them I was doing training in another city for my travel agent job...for five weeks. I ended up calling to tell my father on the bridge before boarding my first working flight, which was to Paris, France. Surprisingly, he took it quite well. I'm sure he was just happy to know I hadn't run off with the circus.

And how about when I announced I was buying my own home? According to my parents, no immigrant son who isn't married needs to leave home. "But we feed you and do your laundry! You have it good you know" were my mother's exact words. My dad just stopped talking for about three weeks.

What about when you tell your parents that big secret you've kept from them about who you are? For me, coming out to my parents was the hardest decision of my life. What made it more difficult was knowing, despite what everyone else said, that they would not accept it (which is a whole other book. That will be my next bestseller: *Being You*).

It was not because I was afraid to come out that I waited until I was thirty-three. It was because I had to be ready to let go of my family.

When I came out to them, it was instant. I was disowned.

How did I let go? I celebrated that I am a unique individual who is not codependent on any other individual.

I reminded myself (hourly) that family is defined only by what I believe to be true.

I redefined what *letting go* even meant. It was now progress, evolution, and self-love.

I chose to give up my need to be accepted. *That* is what I let go, and since then, I've never been more free, more loved, or more clear on my purpose.

Where in your family/relationship life can you choose to let go of your need to be accepted?

_____

_____

_____

By letting go of your need to be accepted, what becomes possible for you?

_____

_____

_____

What can you celebrate right now? (An aha, a realization, or simply a current reality?)

_____

_____

_____

## LETTING GO OF BELIEFS THAT DO NOT SERVE YOU

Exercising letting go over external and family history sets you up for exposing the greatest challenge of all. The challenge of *you*. That is, the challenge that arises when you examine what you believe to be true.

It was one thing to let go of my need for acceptance from my family upon being disowned. It was a whole other challenge to undo over thirty years of programming that had become part of my belief system.

I grew up hearing:

- "You are *nothing* without family."
- "No one will ever treat you as well as we do."
- "Your dreams are for dreamers."
- "Trust no one, not even yourself."
- "I wish we could bring Hitler back to life. The first mission I'd give him would be to exterminate all the gays."

And in the only interaction that happened shortly after I came out to my family:

- "Don't tell anyone. No one needs to know. Just keep it a secret. Live a quiet life, alone."

Undoing all of that programming would take some time and extra muscle.

I remember very clearly in 2011, as I watched my house burn down, thinking, "There is no point...to any of it.... So, if there's no point and no purpose, why can't I just choose to be on-purpose? What if I just decided to *be* the purpose—my life, my ability to connect with others and share my gifts...maybe *that's* it."

Letting go of an entire belief system or even any part of it can be painful. However, I would argue that staying stuck based on what you believe is more painful.

It may sound trite, but I remember having to memorize all the planets in grade school. My teacher gave us the acronym M VEM J SUN P. It served me well, and to this day I've not forgotten it.

Except, back in August of 2006, it was declared that Pluto was not actually a planet. Yes, Pluto was demoted! All of a sudden, everything I believed had to change. I suppose I could have held on and started the *I Believe in Pluto* society.

What beliefs can you let go of that no longer serve you? Perhaps they are ideas you've had since childhood, or things that were imprinted on you that you don't even question today.

_____

_____

_____

By letting go of these beliefs, what becomes possible for you?

_____

_____

_____

What can you celebrate right now?

_____

_____

_____

# LETTING GO

## WHO DO YOU WANT TO BE?

Letting go isn't always easy. Brené Brown teaches that the one thing you should never let go of is who you are. Instead, let go of what other people think—of their expectations and projections.

I've discovered that, again, asking the question "Who do I need/want to be?" serves to support letting go of beliefs that no longer serve you.

I wanted to be free from judgment, free from pain, and free from anxiety. I wanted to be free to be me, to be who I always was.

I want that for you, too. It's the core motivation behind this book, and it's the reason I do what I do for others.

You are ready, now, to become *you*.

To be stripped of beliefs that keep you stuck and small.

What will it take for you to accept the standing ovation that welcomed you into this world?

You are ready, now, to be unburdened!


Who do you want to be?

_____

_____

_____


What beliefs are in the way of you being that person?

_____

_____

_____

How can letting go of those beliefs facilitate you becoming the person you want to be?

_____
_____
_____

By what date will you consider letting go of those beliefs?

_____
_____
_____

What can you celebrate right now?

_____
_____
_____
_____
_____

# SPOTLIGHT: UNAPOLOGETIC INFLUENCER

## UNBURDENED
### BY HEATHER JOY BASSETT

*Heather Joy Bassett is a speaker, author, and mentor. You can learn more about her at HeatherJoyBassett.com.*

Even after years of therapy and personal and professional development, I was not speaking my truth. I was silent and burdened. My quality of life was poor, and it was affecting everyone and everything in my life. It wasn't pretty. Then I began an extraordinary exploration of who I am and why I was living as I was.

Suddenly, I was very aware of the gaps in my life, of what I hadn't taught my children, of my failures and fuckups, and of how I had impacted others.

This realization sent me spiraling into a deeper depression as the guilt burdened me.

Have you ever felt like you are living a lie? I have. It seemed on paper that I had it all! I was the 1986 lacrosse world champion, a successful businesswoman, and a podiatrist. I had a partner, two children, a dog, and even the white picket fence.

Yet I was desperately unhappy, and I couldn't understand why! I was grateful, dutiful, and supporting everyone, but my inner critic was beating me up mercilessly. I was numb. I felt disconnected from my body, my heart, and my soul, and I was apologizing to myself for existing.

Even after doing therapy for decades, I was still stuck, and I couldn't figure out why.

One day, my doctor told me I was being bullied by someone I knew! My body felt this, knew it to be true; the patterns of my behavior and circumstances all fell into place. In that moment, I realized I had not been speaking unapologetically. In fact, I had not spoken my truth for years, unless I was very drunk.

This realization felt like a massive weight being lifted off me. Suddenly, to feel unburdened, to not be lying to myself, went beyond epic to cosmic!

As I took responsibility for the situation I was in, I became unapologetic. I then stood before the people I had thought I was protecting and unapologetically told them of my journey.

The ripples were immediate. Unburdened, my heart began to open. Relief surged through us all. Unapologetic conversations started, and I began to step back into my life.

Today, I no longer have a mental health issue, nor do I take medications or see a therapist. Wow, the power of being unapologetic has been cosmically juicy for me!

Over and over, I have sat in circles with people who have found the courage to speak their truth *out loud and unapologetically*, and the ripples have been immediate. Unburdened, people experience a new lightness. They stand taller, their shoulders relax, the sparkle returns to their eyes, and their hearts begin to open.

Speaking my truth unapologetically has been the most powerful healing modality I have personally experienced.

It is always in the moment when a person has the courage and vulnerability to speak unapologetically that we feel the collective ripples of the unburdened soul and life becomes more magical.

**UN** ARE YOU READY TO BE
UNLEASHED?

# GOING ALL IN

"When something is important enough, you do it even if the odds are not in your favor."

— Elon Musk

In the last chapter, you were invited to flex the muscle called "Letting Go." Letting go is a practice and life skill I really started to research and hone when I got serious about my yoga practice. It quickly became apparent to me that it was nearly impossible to complete a yoga session without letting go of the external world (the to-do lists, work, chores, ideas) and my own limiting beliefs (that my arms may fall off while in Warrior II Pose or that I might fall flat on my face attempting inversions).

By letting go and redefining your relationship with thoughts, beliefs, and even family history, you will be miles closer to achieving what I believe to be your true purpose: being yourself so you can serve others and the world.

The practice of letting go is exactly that, just like in yoga. There is no arrival moment or completion; there is only practice—for life.

I read *The Secret* by Rhonda Byrne when it first swept the world. I had a copy of the book with me during a trip to Los Angeles, and I vividly recall reading through the book while I was enjoying a day at the beach in Santa Monica. With each idea presented in the book, I thought, *Okay, I've been doing that.... I know that.* Essentially, there was nothing *new* in it that I wasn't already doing. Upon completing the book, I said to myself, "But you can't just wish and dream.... I'm all in for being a dreamer, but *I know* you have to actually *do* something about what you want."

As I looked back on my own life, I realized that my biggest successes had included massive action on my part. With each one, I had unleashed sides of myself that I hadn't known existed to that point. I went *all in*!

What will become possible for you when *you* go all in? I've spent my entire life researching this question, even when I didn't know what I was doing.

Certainly, when I was in kindergarten and appointed daily girlfriends, I went all in, and the results, beyond even the benefit of organizing my female fan club, were more confidence and stepping into my role as a leader for the first time.

## COLORING OUTSIDE THE LINES

In my senior year of high school I was invited to spend a summer in Jamaica to set up summer camps and work with some of the poorest communities in Kingston. When I presented the idea to my parents, they laughed and said, "Well, we paid for you to go on the band trip to San Diego last year. If you want to go on this trip, you're going to have to pay for it yourself."

Of course, they fully believed I wouldn't be able to do it, especially since I didn't even have a job at the time.

The opportunity to spend a summer away was as attractive to me then as a new iproduct release is today. I was determined not only to get to Jamaica, but to show my parents I could do it without them.

(Nothing like some good external motivation to inspire an all-in attitude.)

I began studying fundraising, especially in schools. The most obvious choice would be to have a bake sale, the gold standard method to making a buck in a scholastic setting. Everyone loves cake, right?

It quickly became apparent to me, after running the numbers, that a standard bake sale might not get me the funds I needed fast enough. I asked friends, "How much would you pay for a cookie or a slice of cake?" The answers ranged from five to seventy-five cents. I realized that wasn't going to cut it!

The first aha moment for me came when I realized I needed an audience with money: teachers!

The problem: Teachers had rotating lunches, and they didn't all congregate in the same place at the same time.

The solution: I would set up inside or just outside the office, and be there early. Every teacher had to pass by the office to check his or her mail.

The other problem: I knew I couldn't sell enough volume to a teacher who'd spend a minute or less at my baked goods table to raise the funds I needed.

The solution (and big aha): I would have a tasting table where teachers could sample a variety of treats for free (I discovered in my research that teachers loved free stuff) and then place orders for full cakes, treats, and cookies by the dozen!

I went *all in*!

I sequestered the basement kitchen (the typical Italian household has two kitchens, of course) for an entire weekend to bake a variety of cakes and cookies.

Monday morning, I set up just outside the teachers' mailroom.

My bake sale was a hit! Teachers loved that I had created a bake sale just for them. They also loved that they could sample anything for free. It helped that I could actually bake, because within a couple of hours, I had a very long list of orders. Apple Coffee Cake was a big hit, as was my Kahlua Bundt Cake and Chippy Cake. Biscotti were also getting good traction.

I ran my samples table for two days, before school, during breaks, and during lunch.

New Problem: How would I ever bake everything on my own at home?

Solution: Sequester the commercial kitchen at the school that wasn't being used for any class.

Problem: I was still just one person.

Solution: Enroll my friends to become apprentice bakers!

For the next week, a handful of friends and I baked, and baked, and baked.

Of course, when you go from idea to full-blown operation with multiple moving parts in a very short period of time, there are bound to be some misses. Some cakes didn't quite turn out. (In other words, they failed quality control.)

Luckily for me, my experiment and what I was doing started to get attention. I had other students constantly asking me when they would be able to try out the treats!

Aha!

Teenagers will eat anything! During every lunch period, every cake or batch of cookies that didn't pass quality control would be offered to students at a standard bake sale event.

Multiple streams of income!

Ultimately, I raised enough money to get to Jamaica, and in the process, I discovered my entrepreneurial spirit. In fact, the following year, I helped a friend raise money for the same trip by teaching her how to run a similar bake sale extravaganza.

As I reflect back on this memorable moment in my life, I'm pretty sure many of my teachers placed orders simply because they saw how committed I was. And that's the point of this entire chapter.

*Going all in* has some beautiful side-effects. Not only will you move forward toward your dreams, goals, and vision, but you'll also enroll other people into who you are. They will see you as a leader, a trailblazer...a visionary, even. People want to be led by visionaries who are inspiring and who show others what it looks like to be a leader.

Even in my yoga studio business debacle, while most may see that as a failure, I know there was no degree or diploma program that could have taught me more in ten times the amount of time (and investment).

When you commit to going all in, things happen, and people notice.

Take a look at Elon Music and SpaceX.

Thomas Edison and the light bulb.

Even Jesus went all in, which I believe is *the* major contributing factor to the longevity and impact of his story. As I like to joke, 2000 years later, he's still a bestseller!

What will it take for you to go all in?

What is one area in your business or life where you can choose to go all in?

_____

_____

_____

What's holding you back?

_____
_____
_____
_____

What support will you need to go all in? (People, resources, etc.)

_____
_____
_____
_____

What's the very first, most powerful, action you can take toward going all in?

_____
_____
_____
_____

By what date will you take the step to go all in?

_____
_____
_____
_____

## CELEBRATION AS A TOOL

A chapter about going all in would be incomplete without revisiting the element of celebration.

When you decide, hopefully right now, to go all in, take a moment (or several) to celebrate. The act of celebration is a reward that will train your body and mind to want more. You love feeling good. Celebration feels good.

I've never met anyone more expert at celebrating than Joseph McClendon III, the man largely responsible for the success of Tony Robbins' global empire.

I was fortunate enough to meet McClendon at a small two-day experience he was leading that essentially focused on celebration, or as he likes to call it, *asstitude*.

McClendon, a longtime psychologist who's worked with the world's who's who, discovered early in his life that he liked to feel good, and he liked others to feel good, too.

He discovered, and now teaches, the role of your ass in feeling good. As he says, "It's impossible not to feel good when you shake your ass and move your hips around. Try it!"

He's right. I think it's actually physically impossible not to experience a change in mood when you move your hips and shake your behind.

Even though I've spent a lot of my life celebrating things (unintentionally) after the event, I resolved to put this theory to the test. I followed every exercise religiously. It's no accident that the month I started shaking my ass, I had the biggest month I've ever had in my business! I also felt better and had a better mood overall. (Ask my husband; he'll tell you.)

I went so *all in* that to this day, I have people asking me what my secret is. Friends who witnessed it all shaking out (ahem) would call me up to try to figure it out.

My response every time was, "Are you doing the work? Are you fully committed? Are you shaking your ass and celebrating? How many times per day?"

In any given day, I celebrate (vigorously) five to ten times. I even celebrate failures because I enjoy feeling good knowing that I'm still making progress, and having awareness of that fact is, in itself, a reason to celebrate.

How can you incorporate celebration into your daily routine?

Personally, I use the alarm on my phone. Every morning, I check my calendar for appointments. Then I set my alarm to go off between them, at least five to ten times. When the alarm goes off, I shake my ass and acknowledge something I can celebrate. If I'm sitting in my chair (which is often the case), I still shake it—in the chair.

It's almost like pressing a reset button every single time I celebrate. It also produces the unexpected side-effect of not feeling exasperated anytime my phone rings or an alarm goes off. Try it.

When you choose to go all in, combined with regular celebration, you become a magnet for abundance. When you do it despite and against the odds, as Elon Musk teaches us, you position yourself for great things (miracles even) to happen.

How many times per day will you commit to celebrating?

_____

_____

_____

What might get in your way?

_____

_____

_____

_____

How will you manage any obstacles that prevent you from sticking to your new celebration routine?

_____

_____

_____

By when will you start celebrating? (How about right now?)

_____

# SPOTLIGHT: UNAPOLOGETIC INFLUENCER

## UNLEASHED
### BY CHRISTINE GAIL

*Christine Gail is a motivational speaker, leadership coach, publishing and branding coach, and the author of* Unleash Your Rising. *You can learn more about her at UnleashYourRising.com.*

For me, to become unleashed means you are no longer following the crowd. Rather, you have ignited the still quiet voice within that whispers to you that you have a purpose to fulfill...and you fulfill it.

Being unapologetic and unleashed go hand in hand. Becoming unapologetically unleashed requires you to discover your inner truths and then walk with integrity in those truths. It requires purposeful leadership and seeking the collaborative transformation of the world.

Being unleashed, you will begin to take inventory of your intentions and how you lead your life. You will feel prepared to face the ghost stories of your past, to recreate your vision, and to live in the space of conscious creative expression.

Personally, being unleashed has gifted me with the ability to lead with intention in my life and work. I no longer feel limited by a 9-5 job. I show up fully in my creative expression every day in my coaching, writing, and speaking, and as a devoted wife and mother of two spirited girls. In all aspects of my life, I scan my responses to be congruent with peace, love, and connection.

Like everyone else, I have challenging days and periods when things do not go as expected. When that happens, I embrace the role of the student and ask, "What is the lesson in this?" "Where has this shown up elsewhere in my life?" "What were my expectations, and how can I move forward in the flow of what is meant to unfold for me?" I allow the learning to happen rather than covering it up with distraction or doing more. If something comes up from the past, I revisit it in order to release it fully.

I knew at a very young age that I would leave my family and small-town life in Texas to do something bigger than me. It took me years to figure out what that was, and it required revisiting my past where my belief systems and self-worth were first programmed. At the age of four, I experienced abandonment and throughout my entire childhood I felt I had no voice. I later turned that feeling of unworthiness into resiliency. I took the disempowerment I felt and pushed myself to be successful. As a result, I worked and funded myself through college, made six figures right away, then founded and built a multi-million dollar company from the ground up. You would think that for me life was good, but I ended up walking away. I began to listen to the answers that came back to me when I asked, "Am I in integrity with my higher good and am I fulfilling my mission?"

My still inner knowing was activated within me when I began to put my spirituality first and truly listen to the nudges. I became fueled by the motivation to become a conscious, connected mother. I was willing to do whatever it takes to find my own voice, and it led me to inspire others to ignite theirs. I grew the courage to write a book and launched a career that allows me to live life intentionally. The metamorphosis was the hardest part, but all along, I was being directed toward something that better served my mission.

As you embrace being unleashed, you will become a vessel for a message that encourages interconnection and change. You may receive a sign or nudge to take a closer look at your gifts and the gifts of others around you. It may come in the way of revamping how you care for your body, your relationships, and our earth. You may experience a shift in connecting with your family. You may begin to see the bigger picture in your business and in leading your company. This message could come in the way of infusing your story into your business, weaving your personal journey into a book, or enhancing your coaching and speaking platform. After all, we have arrived with an assignment not only to live out our stories, but to share our stories.

The stories of your life are infused with purpose. You may not see the full picture yet of who you are, how you will step into your message, or where your path is leading because you are a painting on the canvas in the making. Living in the flow of creative inspiration will continually unveil the core of who you are and why you are here. As you shift into gratitude and a reverence for your entire journey, your purpose will become unleashed, and it will begin to rise within you like the sun that rises upon the earth to illuminate its beauty and all its gifts.

**UN** ARE YOU READY TO BE
UNBEATABLE?

# KNOWING YOU ARE ALREADY ENOUGH

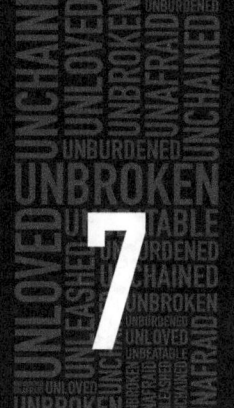

"Courage is resistance to fear, mastery of fear, not absence of fear."

— Mark Twain

In the last chapter, I encouraged you to embrace your visions and dreams and to go all in for them.

Going all in has allowed me to build confidence, friends, followers, and even multiple businesses.

It would be a lie for me to say that going all in solved the issue of fear. In fact, I will go so far as to say you should never try to eliminate all fear. Instead, fear is something to be embraced, negotiated, and danced with.

Especially in speaking and leading, fear is a topic that comes up with every single student, client, or performer I've ever worked with. When it does, I encourage it, and I let people know I'd be more concerned if they had no fears about speaking, leading, or performing. For me, that would indicate that the stakes weren't high enough and that they didn't care enough.

## INVESTIGATING FEAR

Understanding fear is something that has become an obsession for me. For many years, I've wondered what fear actually is, and how to truly master it, as Mark Twain suggests in his famous quote.

When I was completing one of my early yoga teacher training courses, I witnessed what some might call a miracle. It was a moment that forever changed the way I approached fear.

I was attending a teacher training in the Catskills of New York State. The training included a lot of physical practice as well as several in-class and discussion sessions.

The leader, renowned yogi Baron Baptiste, would often invite people to the microphone to share breakthroughs, questions, and aha moments.

During a mic session, one woman stepped up to the mic and immediately started blurting out, "Oh, my gosh, I'm so nervous…. I never do this…. I can't believe it…. I'm feeling so scared! I don't know if I can speak!"

She was speaking fast and furiously, but Baptiste gently interrupted her with a boyish smile and said, "Hang on…you feel scared? Tell me more. Can you describe exactly what you're feeling?"

Woman: My heart is racing. I'm sweating, and I feel it all up here. [Motions toward her chest.]

Baron: Where exactly in your chest, and what exactly are you feeling?

Woman: It's all here [motions toward her chest] and it's tight….

Baron: Is it constricting? Is it in one specific area?

Woman: I feel it's like a ball near my heart.

Baron: Okay, is it at the surface? One-inch deep?

Woman: Um…it's just under the surface.

# KNOWING YOU ARE ALREADY ENOUGH

Baron: How big is it? Size of a grapefruit? A tennis ball? Ping pong ball?

Woman: It's the size of a grapefruit...no...an orange...hmm, no...a lemon.... wait...actually, I don't feel anything—I'm fine!

What sorcery had I just witnessed?

Baron was at least ten feet away from the woman, and she was standing all by herself at the microphone. He never approached her. I and a room full of students (over one hundred of us) was watching the exchange from our seats.

Baron had simply asked her some clarifying questions and used her initial admission of feeling afraid as an opportunity to investigate.

## FEAR IS OPPORTUNITY

I have spoken on many podcasts and been interviewed about fear a lot. Each time, I always say, "Fear is an opportunity." And so it is. It's an opportunity to look deeper at what the actual fear is or is not.

Often when fear arises, we believe it. Fear is tricky, and it feeds off our highly suggestible imaginations.

The woman at the yoga training couldn't even verbalize what she was afraid of. As Baron probed, she began to realize her fear was just a sensation. She may as well have been describing that she felt in love because the description would have been quite similar.

It seems to me that fear always comes down to one of two things: fear based on beliefs (history) or fear of the unknown (survival instinct).

The latter is the most common and covers a whole range of fears. Fear of rejection, fear of failure, fear of success, fear of looking bad.... All of these fears occur when you imagine an outcome that hasn't yet come to pass (and may never come to pass), but you decide that if that outcome should be realized, you would not be able to cope. So fear keeps you safe (and alive).

Many of the speakers and leaders I work with deal with fear at some level. Many of them actually delay their own development based on fear. They'll tell me, "I'm not ready to do a TEDx talk," "I can't apply for that speaking opportunity because I'm afraid I'm not fully qualified," or "I'm not ready to speak in front of a large crowd yet."

In each of these scenarios, the fears are not grounded in any concrete evidence; rather, they are based on *what if* scenarios.

I always encourage people to do things they don't believe they are qualified for. Let the people who are making the final selection determine whether you're qualified or not. Just go all in!

There's a great story about one of the piano players on *The Lawrence Welk Show*.

Jo Ann Castle replied to a casting call looking for experienced piano entertainers who had a large repertoire of ragtime music.

She applied despite only knowing a single ragtime tune. Instead of surrendering to her fear, she used it as an opportunity to learn her first ragtime piece.

On audition day, she wowed the panel and was ultimately hired. She worked hard her entire career on the show to learn more and more ragtime pieces and many others for each show. The opportunity to become a household name only became available to her because she chose to see fear as an opportunity for personal growth.

Fear based on beliefs and history can be difficult to overcome—especially when you are able to prove a reason for being fearful, such as, "The last time I spoke in front of an audience, I forgot what I was going to say, so I never want to do that again."

My question is then, "What about that one time you fell off your bike, or the hundreds of times you tried to take a step when you were an infant and fell, or the time you were learning to speak and used the wrong word or didn't know the right word?"

It seems to me that you overcame fear in all those situations. In fact, you used those situations as the opportunity to master a new skill, and in the process, master your fear.

## YOU ARRIVED FEARLESS

The great Dr. Wayne Dyer talks about a theory he has in his book (and the movie) *The Shift*. He muses about how our time in the womb is simple and abundant. Things are easy. We simply surrender as a fetus, and abundance comes. He goes on to state, "Why then do things need to change when we arrive in this world?"

Infants are fearless. As an infant, you act on intuition (albeit, at times, the intuition may get you hurt; that's what parents are for). The more you learn and know, the more fear becomes a guiding force in life.

What if you just moved through decision making from a place of "I don't know everything" to "I have some history in this area, but I don't know what will happen this time, so I'll just try and see"? Then you would be open to the adventure of the experience rather than fearing the outcome.

Here's the other thing: Why are you stopping yourself before you even know the outcome of something? I'm not saying you should go out and skydive and bungee jump and crush all your bucket list fears. I'm talking about tackling everyday opportunities that align you with your purpose.

## WHAT ARE YOU MORE AFRAID OF?

Sometimes we have to look at the alternative to letting our fear take control. As an example, let me share a story about Tina, who signed up for a full-day workshop with me.

Tina was terrified of speaking in front of an audience. In fact, when it came time to say a few words in front of the group (there were five other people in the room, including me), she fought me.

Tina helps people as they age to make informed decisions when it comes to their care so they can age with dignity and not become a burden to anyone. It's a *very* personal topic for her because she was blessed to support her own grandparents as they aged and then passed with grace, surrounded by loved ones at home.

Sadly, that is not the norm. She's witnessed so many elderly people slip through the cracks of the healthcare system and end up alone. She's also seen families left with big burdens after their loved ones died.

I asked Tina, "What are you more afraid of: speaking and saving people's lives, or staying silent while so many others live in pain, die alone, and cause grief for their families?"

That comment was enough for Tina to get on stage and speak, and she hasn't stopped since. Today, she runs a very successful and growing aging lifecare business.

What is possible for you on the other side of fear?

As I tell everyone I work with, the world is waiting for you! When are you going to choose to speak and lead like you were meant to?

When you discover that fear truly is the opportunity to expand and grow, a whole new world of possibility opens up.

What is the dominant fear keeping you small in some area of your life or business?

_____

_____

_____

_____

What opportunity is available to you on the other side of your fear (when you master your fear in this situation)?

_____
_____
_____
_____

What support do you need to master this fear?

_____
_____
_____
_____

By when will you take action on the opportunity to master this fear?

_____
_____
_____
_____

Discovery takes time. You may need to reread these first seven chapters multiple times to discover fully your unapologetic edge and who you truly are.

Remember, it's in *who* you are (and who you've always been) that you'll unearth your passions, your purpose, your message as a speaker, and your platform as a leader.

Discovery is a lifelong practice. Commit to discovering yourself daily (and celebrate)!

What are you celebrating right now?

_____

_____

_____

_____

_____

# SPOTLIGHT: UNAPOLOGETIC INFLUENCER

## UNBEATABLE

**BY RANDY MOLLAND**

*Randy Molland is a speaker, influencer, and investor. You can learn more about him on social media @RandyMolland or at RandyMolland.com.*

My definition of unbeatable is someone who has been through his or her toughest times and turned that tragic experience into a positive message. When you are unbeatable, you are in charge of your mind and not giving in even when you are at your worst.

Being unapologetic in relation to being unbeatable is all about how you can take some of the toughest situations there are and be grateful for the strength they have given you as you grow from them. I am unapologetic about how grateful I am for the opportunity that came from losing my brother and best friend. Rather than let those experiences break me apart, I have used them to build the type of person I have become. They have helped me become unbeatable in life, and to share my story to help enlighten others who are struggling through their situations. Today, I use that experience as motivation to create the lifestyle *they* always deserved but never got to have. Being unbeatable has pushed me to learn how to use my brain and emotions in ways I never knew existed, and I am now creating a massive impact because of it.

I want others to change the way we think about tragic incidents. We have a choice in how we want to handle situations. It's our choice to let them tear us down, but it is also our choice to let them be the most powerful things in the world. Nothing I can do can reverse what happened or bring them back, but I can take the lessons I've learned from these experiences and use them to inspire others and create a legacy in their names.

First, I lost my little brother to SIDS (Sudden Infant Death Syndrome) when I was just three years old. Although I can't remember much about the event, it had a drastic impact on my family and my upbringing. I was bullied and teased for crying in class my entire school career, and today, I openly cry in public when I share the story with others about how my parents took the tragedy and used it to raised my brother and me with great respect, passion, devotion, and unconditional love. My parents never gave up preaching to us about how important family, loving, and caring were. They are a living testament to how someone can be unbeatable in the hardest of times, and I love to share what their example has done for my life.

Then, at age twenty-four, I lost my best friend, mentor, and future business partner through a tragic job site accident. Remembering how my parents had used their loss to create a positive situation for my brother and me, I decided I would turn losing my friend into an opportunity to make a positive impact on everyone around me and, eventually, as many people as I could reach.

I am now on a journey to inspire others to go bigger with their dreams and stories so they can be more generous with their lives. It is called the Go Big to Give Big movement. The mission behind it is to allow others to feel unapologetic about creating success because the more success we create, the bigger the impact we can have on the world and others around us.

My friend used to tell me every single day, "Why did you come to work today? You have so much potential that you're not using. You need to go do something bigger than just being on this jobsite." He would tell me that not just once or twice, but every single day. So when he passed, there was only one thing to do—go find my true potential. I have since fallen in love with this journey in a way I never dreamed. I left my job and co-founded multiple companies that have for-purpose models built into them, which have allowed me to give back to charities, pursue my dream of speaking on stage, travel across North America meeting like-minded people, and create a lifestyle of freedom and enjoyment while doing so. All of this has been fueled by telling the stories of what I have overcome so others can also learn how to live an unbeatable life.

By being unbeatable, I have been able to create a company whose mission is to help one million people become financially educated and invested in real estate so they can start living more fulfilled lives. Being unbeatable has allowed me to show others how to push through adversity and look at things in a different way. What if the reason we lose someone is so we can go help a hundred others? If you can't fix what has happened, why let it break you? If you become unbeatable, then you can use that to make a bigger impact.

I have now used both of these experiences of loss that could "beat" a person to become unbeatable and to empower others to take things that are normally life-changing tragic events and rewire their brains to learn how to make them their most impactful experiences and be unapologetic about their happiness in life because of them.

Imagine if we took the toughest situations that can send people spiraling into depression, alcoholism, drug addiction, and even suicide, and we used them to help those same people come out of the situations not only stronger, but able to handle situations going forward with ease. Being unbeatable is a life skill; it's something that, if you can learn to handle it, can be the most powerful thing in the world. It's controlling your mind instead of letting your mind control you. It's reprogramming your brain to understand that if you can't change a situation, you can change how you perceive it. Here's a quote I read regularly that has helped me to change my perspective:

> "You either get bitter or you get better. It's that simple. You either take what has been dealt to you and allow it to make you a better person, or you allow it to tear you down. The choice does not belong to fate. It belongs to you."
>
> — Josh Shipp

If I were not unbeatable, I honestly think I would be in a horrible state right now, or even worse, not even here. By learning my whole life to look at the positive and always try to find the light in every situation, I have been able to grow and learn to handle tough situations. Today, I take every curve ball thrown at me and find a way to turn it into a home run. Yes, it's that simple. By using positive thinking and looking at situations as opportunities, instead of being a victim, I am able to create an unbeatable lifestyle that is infectious to those around me. I can unapologetically say that I am grateful to have lost such amazing people in my life because it is now allowing me to become the best version of myself, to live a fulfilled life, and to teach others how they can thrive in the wake of misfortune.

I encourage you to become unbeatable and use all your misfortunes to create a life that will allow you to use your full potential.

*Dedicated to my brother, Dean Molland, and best friend, Rob Davison. I promise to use my full potential and live a fulfilled life big enough for all of us.*

# PART II
# DEVELOPING YOUR LEADERSHIP SKILLS

**UN** ARE YOU READY TO BE
UNBREAKABLE?

# ACCOUNTABILITY

> "There's been nothing but discipline,
> discipline, discipline all my life."
>
> — Celine Dion

The first seven chapters of this book focused solely on discovery of who you are and why you are who you are to uncover your speaking brand, your idea worth spreading, and your leadership style.

Most people, including successful ones, make the mistake of skipping the discovery phase, or they don't spend enough time in discovery.

Over the years, I've made the observation that once people move from discovery to development, most further discovery ceases. In other words, a common mistake is to think on something, have an aha moment, and then run with it, developing and delivering it to the world.

Sometimes, it works. Other times, you may find yourself up to your eyeballs in a project wondering, *How did I get to this point?* I certainly felt that way with my yoga studio business. Once I set my sights on the goal, nothing could have derailed me. In fact, I ignored new discoveries (the red flags that would have caused me to *abort mission*) because I was so focused on developing my idea and bringing it to life, no matter what.

How do you stay in discovery even when you're developing an idea? How do you remain present, open, and in alignment with who you are?

In this chapter, you will learn the one thing that made all the difference for me when I first immigrated to the United States from Canada. The one thing that people thought was my unique element—my gift, when, in fact, it was something I had to practice daily, and still do to this day.

## RADICAL ACCOUNTABILITY

Accountability is no big secret, so you may feel inclined to rush through this chapter or skip it altogether. I advise you not to. The kind of accountability I'm sharing with you is, shall we say, radical and even unconventional. (More on being unconventional in the next chapter.)

The standard accountability model would have you set goals or tasks that you check off as each is completed. Perhaps you even have a buddy, a coach, or some sort of device in place that allows you to stay on track, motivated, and supported.

Being a pretty strong Type A personality, I love my lists, and I'm pretty methodical about getting things done. The only thing that gets in my way is that I'm hyper-creative, which means I'm often juggling multiple idea balls at the same time.

Despite being an entrepreneur in some form or another my entire life, when I moved to the United States, I started exploring coaching programs so I could get the support I needed to recreate my past successes.

I suppose it's not our fault that we aren't the greatest at being self-accountable. Our Western society's model—go to school, get a job, buy a home, get married, have kids, etc.—doesn't fully develop the skill of being accountable; rather, it trains us as followers.

# ACCOUNTABILITY

Every program I looked into and became a part of had some sort of accountability process in place. Some executed it better than others; however, in the end, no one was directly teaching self-accountability and how intrinsic it is to success.

I've come to learn that creating goals and tasks does not develop accountability, even when you attach "by when" dates and have a buddy to keep you in integrity with what you say you're going to do and achieve.

One program I signed up for was a six-month coaching program called Accelerate. It was created by Nick Unsworth of Life on Fire. (You'll read about his unwavering faith in Chapter 12). I was ready to accelerate so it was a no-brainer decision to sign up.

I was paired up with a buddy, became part of a small power group of six others, and was assigned a coach I would speak to for thirty minutes every Monday and Friday. Every Monday, Wednesday, and Friday, I'd fill out accountability forms where I would identify the goal I had for the week, the progress I was making toward my bigger six-month goal, and the questions that would support me in getting clear on the direction I was taking.

You can imagine that, what with filling out three forms every week, getting on two coaching calls, one additional small group call on Wednesday, and all the other times spent supporting a buddy, it was a busy six months. I was quite vocal in my opinions of all the *busy work* involved, but because I had paid a handsome sum for the coaching, I surrendered to the process and just did everything asked of me, even when I hated doing it.

## UNPRECEDENTED ACCOUNTABILITY

Every week during those six months, I had to come up with a goal that was unprecedented (something I had never done before) and measurable. For instance, having a goal of feeling good about myself didn't count because there was no way to measure it. The goal of feeling good about myself because I had three new paying clients sign up would be acceptable. The next week, if I wanted to get more clients, the goal would have to be more than three (unprecedented). You get the picture.

In the third month of the program, my coach Jenn challenged me to attach a monetary figure to my weekly goal because I had expressed my dislike for making money a goal. I kept arguing that money didn't motivate me, which is a huge mindset problem when you're an entrepreneur.

I was so irritated with Jenn pressing me on this issue that I decided to create an outlandish goal for the week. I declared that I would make $20,000 in that week. It was completely unprecedented because I'd never made that amount on my own in such a short period of time, and it was certainly measurable.

In my mind, I pretty much knew I wouldn't achieve this goal, *but* I decided to go all in anyway, if for no other reason than to prove Jenn and the whole process wrong.

I had the goal, the accountability, the coach....

Can you guess what happened?

I didn't make a dime that week.

I'm sure Jenn dreaded getting on the call on Friday with me, probably expecting me to say, "See! It doesn't work!"

I'm also positive she was floored when I started out our call as happy as if I'd won the lottery.

"What are you celebrating today?" she asked.

"I figured it out! I totally get it now!" I replied.

On the weekly forms was a section that asked "Who do you need to be in order to achieve your goal?" Responses like "confident," "organized," "diligent," and "focused" would fill in the section.

Here's what I figured out: It wasn't about the goals at all. How can you really be accountable to a goal, something you have no idea whether you'll be able to hit anyway? You can, however, be accountable to yourself. That is, to who you are being.

As I described my epiphany to Jenn on our call, I said, "I became an animal this week. I didn't recognize myself. I've never been so driven, so unmessable, so committed to being myself! In fact, I was pretty detached from the outcome but totally in tune with myself. I've never felt so confident and so on purpose in my life!"

## ACCOUNTABILITY TO WHO YOU ARE BEING

Radical accountability, then, is being accountable to who you are being in the process of achieving. Because I was accountable to the personality traits I knew I would have to have in order to pull off a multi-five-figure week, I learned a great deal about myself. I especially learned how I show up in the world normally versus how I need to show up to build the kind of success I want to build for my life and for all the people I want to support.

Being accountable to who you are being is the key. Most programs and coaches out there tend to focus on the *doing*, and even those coaches who have done a great deal of transformational work and understand *being* first is the key still focus on goals and measurable progress.

You might be wondering why I'm celebrating the fact that I didn't achieve my goal, not even close. The real celebration was the realization that in the most successful moments of my life, it was the way I showed up that was the constant. The same was true for the not-so-successful moments.

During the high school bake sale for my Jamaica trip, I had been innovative, creative, enterprising, bold, and unstoppable.

In pitching to a major television network and being told "That was the best pitch we've ever seen," I had been audacious, confident, true to myself, collaborative, and unapologetic in the way we pitched (despite warnings from our executive producer that what we were going to do would put off TV executives).

In leaving my secure teaching job and immigrating to the United States without a plan, I had been confident, open, creative, committed, and unwavering.

The pattern became clear. It wasn't in the actions I took, the goals I achieved, or the money I made where I found success. Time and time again, it was who I was being that led to success and a greater sense of fulfillment. The more committed (obsessed, in fact) I was to a *way of being*, the more success I would experience.

## WHO ARE YOU WILLING TO BE?

What about highly successful people at the top of their game? Who is the Dalai Lama being day-to-day? Or Richard Branson, Oprah Winfrey, Ellen DeGeneres…? How about people like Jesus, Gandhi, or Nelson Mandela? What about Michael Jackson, Celine Dion, Prince, or Dolly Parton?

Henry Ford once said, "A business that makes nothing but money is a poor business." I believe (and know) the same to be true for individuals.

Walt Disney said, "Disneyland is a work of love. We didn't go into Disneyland just with the idea of making money."

Steve Jobs said, "Being the richest man in the cemetery doesn't matter to me. Going to bed at night saying we've done something wonderful, that's what matters to me."

# ACCOUNTABILITY

Success doesn't come by chance, nor does it happen based on setting an external goal to be successful, make money, or even make a difference. While some of these elements are part of success, I know firsthand that none of these thing are real motivators. Feeling good is the motivator. Feeling in alignment, on-purpose, and meaningful motivate us to greatness. The way to feeling good is through radical commitment to being the person who feels good about who he or she is being. No, that's not a puzzle.

Think about it. Who do you need to be in order to feel good about yourself? Most people, when answering this question, revert to things that are external. However, "I need to be successful" is not a way of being; it's a byproduct.

Take no more than sixty seconds to brainstorm a list. Who do you need to be in order to feel good about yourself?

_____

_____

_____

_____

_____

_____

_____

_____

_____

_____

Think back to all your successes. Who were you being leading up to creating the success? Describe yourself, the personality traits, the drive—who were you in that moment?

| Successful moment | Who were you being? |
| --- | --- |
| _____ | _____ |
| _____ | _____ |
| _____ | _____ |
| _____ | _____ |

Do you see how your *being* is a big part of the whole success equation? The most successful speakers, leaders, thought leaders, artists, and performers have a way about them, and so do you. When you commit to *being* you, unapologetically, you are more in alignment with yourself and your purpose, and success follows.

Do you want to know what happened in the weeks after I had my big aha moment with coach Jenn? I had my first-ever, self-generated, five-figure week, and my first-ever, multiple-five-figure month! Just as Celine Dion is quoted as saying in the opening of this chapter, it took discipline, a lot of it, and it still does. I remind myself every day, multiple times per day, who I am and who I need to be, and I celebrate!

If you feel there are areas in which you can still achieve your ideal dream life, imagine what could become possible when you confidently become more of who you are, just like your favorite successful speaker, leader, visionary, or celebrity.

ACCOUNTABILITY

What will you do to be more accountable to yourself?

_____
_____
_____

By when will you start?

_____
_____
_____

What are you celebrating right now?

_____
_____
_____
_____
_____
_____

# SPOTLIGHT: UNAPOLOGETIC INFLUENCER

## UNBREAKABLE
**BY KAT HALUSHKA**

*Kat Halushka is an international speaker and meetup queen. You can learn more about her at KatHalushka.com.*

For me, being unbreakable means "I can. I will. Nothing can stop me." It's being myself and not letting anything or anyone be in the way of my dreams. It's conquering every failure, ignoring every dig someone throws my way, and overcoming every "what if" in the back of my mind.

I learned to be unbreakable when I immigrated to Canada from Russia. I only knew a few words of English, had no friends here, and didn't know what to do next. That almost broke me—actually, it did break me. I refused to move on with my life but instead became stuck in my past, obsessed with going back to the known and the comfortable. But that wasn't an option, so every day was hell and every moment empty. But the desire to see my friends again drove me into two full-time jobs and forced me to adapt. That was really my first introduction into creating the unbreakable me! Having a goal was what made me learn my first 100 English words, and so what if they were "Welcome to Tim Hortons" and "double-double"—it was a start.

There would be many more failures in my future: trying to get a diploma without money, my first relationship, starting a business, my first client to request a refund.... But as long as I had a goal, nothing could knock me down. I just kept getting up, dusting myself off, and trying again.

Fast forward to now. I have to say, business has to be one of the best ways to build an unbreakable personality. Hundreds of "Nos" and thousands of hours of work with, sometimes, still not getting to the dream definitely build character. But it does get easier to get up after being knocked down by life. And every time, that getting-up muscle becomes stronger until getting up is just part of the process.

Therefore, I say to you, "Train that unbreakable muscle!" Get out of your comfort zone even if it's just a little bit, even if it's only once a month. Whatever that means to you. It could be getting on stages, cold calling your dream client, inviting that cute girl/guy out for a dinner.... Do it! Today happens only once—don't waste it! I promise you won't break if you try. In fact, you'll just become even more unbreakable.

**UN** ARE YOU READY TO BE
UNCONVENTIONAL?

# EMBRACING DIFFERENT AS NORMAL

# 9

> "There was no one near to confuse me, so
> I was forced to become original."
>
> — Joseph Haydn

In the last chapter, I shared with you a key element, the secret, if you will, to success in every area of your life. It's so simple that most people (in my own research, less that 10 percent) will never adopt self-accountability for who they are being.

Before I take on any client or project, I always give a bit of a disclaimer. I'm interested in working with people who are up to something bigger than increasing their income or influence. I'm only interested in working with those willing to become themselves and who aren't afraid to be challenged to stretch, evolve, shed, and grow into truly becoming unapologetic about who they are, why they are who they are, and how they want to inspire others to do the same.

In this chapter, I challenge you to do the same. What would become possible for you if you became radically you? What would become possible if you were to say the things you really wanted to say? (For positive transformation of others, not just to speak for the sake of speaking. As I remind all my speaking clients, "No one actually cares about you or your story. They are too busy caring about themselves. Speak to transform them so they can, in turn, transform the world.") What would be possible for you if you became open and genuinely confident in your mission and vision? What would become possible if today became the day you started to pave your own way?

**BEING UNCONVENTIONAL**

In Chapter 3, I mentioned the time I pitched a television show to a major network.

Everything about what we were doing was unconventional. From the idea to the execution, and even the pitch itself.

We teamed up with an experienced television producer for this project because without someone with credits, getting a major TV deal is a more difficult proposition.

We spent months preparing the show bible, log line, concept, segments, music, and bigger vision.

The idea was big—something that had never been done before on television.

I'll never forget the look on our executive producer's face when we said, "We are going to sing and dance in the pitch to the network."

I thought he was going to fall out of his chair. He advised us that doing so would be a bad idea, that no one really does that in the industry, at least not when you're doing a first pitch.

Having come from the world of theater, we had no idea how to nor any interest in conforming to the standards of the industry considering the show we were pitching was like nothing that had ever existed, and it was a musical show concept.

Sometimes, being naive is a good thing. Just as the Joseph Hayden quote above states, if you aren't influenced by others, you can create your own path. Hayden didn't do too badly following that advice considering that he's still regarded as one of the greatest innovators of classical music form and style.

Much to our executive producer's dismay, we did sing and dance in the network executives' office, as the rest of the network's team (it was a mostly open concept space) listened, I'm sure.

The result? The top executive in charge of programming said, "That was the best pitch we've ever seen! Wow!"

A few weeks later, we got official word. We didn't get a green light because "We don't believe people want to see kids singing and dancing on TV."

The Ryan Murphy television phenomenon *Glee* came out a few years later. Apparently, people *did* want to see kids singing and dancing on TV.

We were unconventional and it got us noticed. We were actually invited to repitch other concepts and set up future meetings.

When I think back to the path I followed in my most successful moments, I was not following the crowd. I don't want to insinuate that you should never follow someone else's lead. There are people who have paved the way for us, and there are certain standards in some industries that simply work.

If you want to get a pop song on the radio, it has to be within a certain length, with a musical introduction of a certain length, and a soaring chorus. There are exceptions, of course, but the vast majority of songs accepted fit this pattern.

## MARCHING TO THE BEAT OF YOUR OWN DRUM

After my house burned down in 2011, I was faced with the task of rebuilding my home and my life. For anyone who's built a home before, you know what goes into it. It is practically a full-time job. I was building my home while still working my full-time job. Luckily, my home was very close to the school I taught at.

Thousands of decisions are required to bring a home to life from the ground up. Overall design and layout, where to locate ducts and electrical, quality of finishes, colors, appliances, countertops, door hardware, etc.

This was a rare opportunity to oversee every detail since I was working with my contractor personally. We had a great relationship, and I can actually say that most of the process was fun.

I did, however, have to fight for what I wanted every step of the way. Why? Because I was taking an unconventional route.

Because the loss in the fire was so extreme, I knew I was going to build a home that would maximize a return should I ever decide to sell.

I started becoming known as "Prince Davide" to the building crew, not because I was high maintenance, but because the choices I was making were not standard, from mixing hickory with raw travertine, to the kinds and colors of paint I wanted to use. I even took it upon myself to purchase all the smaller finishes (toilets, plumbing fixtures, lighting fixtures, and appliances) myself.

At every meeting (every few days), a typical interaction sounded like this:

Contractor: We're ready for flooring.

Me: Great, I've chosen a natural hickory that will cover the entire upstairs, and two rooms on the main floor. The rest of the main floor will be 16" x 16" travertine, no special thresholds. I want the two surfaces to come together seamlessly.

Contractor: I wouldn't do that if I were you.

Me: Why?

# EMBRACING DIFFERENT AS NORMAL

Contractor: No one ever does that.... I don't think it's going to look good.

Me: I'll take my chances.

When all was said and done and the crew came over to hand me the keys, the project manager said, "You know, I gotta say, I really didn't believe in your vision for this home. Your choices are so unique, and I was afraid your combinations and even room layout choices were a mistake.... I was wrong. You've built a beautiful home!"

My commitment to being unconventional paid off. A few years later, when I sold the home, the closing price reflected the success of my choices.

Are you willing to be unconventional, without influence from others when it comes to your vision?

Imagine how history might have been different if Walt Disney had decided to follow standard theme park conventions in his Disneyland and Disney World designs?

One of my favorite stories of Disney is how he had to take an unconventional approach when he was purchasing the land for Disney World in Florida.

As the story goes, Walt knew that if local authorities saw one person purchasing large areas of land (despite the land being swamp), they would raise the prices because it would indicate that someone (Walt) had figured out a way to develop the land.

The workaround Walt came up with was to make a few smaller purchases over a period of time using dozens of "dummy" corporations. (My favorite was named the M. T. Lott Corporation. Get it? Empty Lot!) That way, nothing would get traced back (too easily) to the man who was already well known for Disneyland.

Thanks to his foresight and unconventional approach to solving the problem, Walt purchased the land he needed. Twenty-seven-thousand acres of land was purchased from $80 to $80,000 per acre. (Of course, prices increased as it became clear there was interest in the area.)

Furthermore, Walt's vision was so unique that Disney World was mostly built and brought to life *after* his death. Unconventional is remembered. Walt's unconventional vision for a park that suited children and families playing and having fun together enrolled dedicated followers who made it their mission to bring the project to life as Walt would have wished.

## WHO ARE YOU WILLING TO BE?

How about Elon Musk, Richard Branson, Mother Teresa...all of them chose unconventional paths, and one could say they all have had unconventional personalities.

Are you willing to discover who you truly are by putting on the blinders and just *being*—by leading others with innovation and inspiration and positively influencing transformation?

Joseph Haydn is regarded as the greatest innovator of classical form, the father of the symphony (he wrote 107), and the creator of the string quartet. Because he was not overly influenced by any other great composers (he wasn't mentored by any of the prominent greats; in fact, he was Beethoven's teacher for a time!), he didn't suffer from comparanoia, so he was able to discover his own way, develop it, and deliver his vision and legacy to the world.

## COMPARANOIA

When I immigrated to the United States, I had the opportunity to become a student again. Because I couldn't legally work for a period of time, I looked at what other people were doing in the speaking and leadership space.

# EMBRACING DIFFERENT AS NORMAL

Over and over, there was one thing I kept hearing. "If you want to be successful in this world, especially in the digital realm, you must deliver value!" I'm going to tackle the whole *value* argument in a later chapter; however, I want to address one aspect of this right now.

As I demonstrated earlier, when I do something, I go all in. To become a speaker, I did everything I was told, including:

- Get a website
- Start a blog
- Do Facebook advertising
- Get a ChatBot
- Have a Facebook business page
- Have a Twitter account
- Have a LinkedIn account
- Have an Instagram account
- Have a YouTube channel
- Design a course
- Have a lead magnet
- Have a funnel
- Go networking
- Get on podcasts
- Get branded
- Get published on major media outlets

The list could go on for several pages.

I did all of it, exactly as I was told.

I also started to pay attention to people in the speaking sphere and how they had built their businesses. What I discovered was very troubling.

My purpose in sharing this is simply an observation. I'm not here to throw anyone under the bus or to expose anything scandalous. I just want to shine the light on what's going on out there in the hopes that you will take a more critical approach to bringing your own vision to life!

Some are business coaches who use speaking as a way to build their businesses.

Some are artists, musicians, or performers of some kind.

All have a "formula" for writing a talk or converting from the stage to bring you *at least* a 10x return.

Most "speaker coaches" are not professional speakers at all.

Most are not even great speakers, actually.

The ones who are good speakers usually do not have a background in coaching or teaching others.

All make near-extravagant claims of their and their clients' success.

Do you really believe that following someone else's "formula" will bring you the same success?

## BLAZING YOUR OWN TRAIL

In my study of world leaders, performers, speakers, artists, and beyond, I have not seen one case where the ingénue has risen to the level of the master in an identical way. It simply doesn't happen.

More common, however, is seeing people become victims of comparanoia while their guru coaches dismiss their mediocre progress by saying, "Well, you didn't do everything I said, exactly."

# EMBRACING DIFFERENT AS NORMAL

What if you were to put the blinders on and give yourself a very limited amount of time to stay in tune with your industry? Then, you take a look at the data you've collected and you begin to ask yourself what you believe and how you want to deliver your vision to your audience.

I assure you Elon Musk isn't *waiting* to see what his competitors do to take action, and I encourage you not to wait either.

Be unconventional. Someone is waiting for your "breath of fresh air" approach in a sea of sameness. I can't guarantee you'll be successful on the first try, but I can guarantee you'll begin to attract 100 percent of your ideal audience, the followers who love you, and your tribe that you will eventually lead in your own way. You have to start, though, with who you are being. *That* will get you noticed for the long term.

Where in your business or life do you feel you are following someone else's lead?

_____

_____

_____

What would it look like for you to do it your own way? (Brainstorm your ideas.)

_____

_____

_____

Who do you need to be in order to take your unconventional path?

_____

_____

_____

What's the most important first step you will take to set the wheels in motion?

_____

_____

_____

By what date will you take the first steps on your new path?

_____

_____

_____

# SPOTLIGHT: UNAPOLOGETIC INFLUENCER

## UNCONVENTIONAL
**BY MILANA LESHINSKY**

*Milana Leshinsky is an entrepreneur, the queen of simplicity, and the inventor of Telesummit. You can learn more about her at Milana.com.*

Being unconventional is not easy. It's uncomfortable and scary at times to challenge the way things have been done for many years. Although it may work for the "elite minority"—the top 5 percent, the most influential people in the industry—the rest of the people are left struggling and floundering. It takes courage not only to notice this, but to bring attention to it and try to find a solution that may go against accepted conventions.

Not everyone has the courage or cares enough to be unconventional. Most people go with the flow. It's easier and safer. It's risky to question publicly something that the top 5 percent have enjoyed and profited from for years. An unconventional approach doesn't mean having the answers or the solution. But simply shining the light on an issue can open up a conversation about how it can be done differently, better, and, ultimately, in a way that benefits the majority.

We all need to feel the fear and do it anyway. Question. Challenge. Share your unconventional ideas. You will attract other advocates of your message and will come up with a solution faster.

The other choice is to remain conventional, but that's just too boring. Doing things the same way everyone else is doing them doesn't allow for fresh innovative solutions.

A few years ago I left a seven-figure business I had built with a business partner. At first, I was at a loss. I had no deadlines, no meetings, nothing to launch, nothing to grow. I felt like an entrepreneur without a business. But then I started seeing that I hadn't just walked away from a business. I walked away from a "conventional" way of growing a company and becoming successful in my industry. I suddenly saw that there's a better way to do things. It may be a less common, less popular, less accepted way. It's unconventional, and because of that, it will receive more criticism—but it will have more impact.

By leaving my company, I had some time to reflect on our industry and see it the way the majority of people were experiencing it. And it was a truly eye-opening experience. I saw that the strategies that work for people at the top don't really work for people at the bottom. In other words, the methods taught by successful entrepreneurs will often be ineffective for those new to online entrepreneurship. Those methods require skills, reputation, credibility, and experience—things that take time to acquire. That's why when I discovered the way of simplicity-driven entrepreneurship, I knew it contained the key to success for those who've struggled to get their business off the ground in the coach, author, and speaker space.

"Grow with what you know"—that's the idea behind a simplicity-based business. Yes, you can learn all the marketing, sales funnels, and automation strategies, and you can build a team.... But all in time. Start where you are now.

I think I've always looked for unconventional, unique, innovative ideas. It might be rooted in my music training background, where we were challenged to create our own harmonies, break out of the ordinary, and create unexpected, unordinary sounds. In business, I always look for something that's not been done before because that's how you stand out. Ordinary ideas just don't inspire me—I crave something different, unique, unordinary, and unconventional.

Ultimately, don't play "follow the leader," the leader being anyone who positions him- or herself as a guru. A guru is not always right. Don't let anyone tell you that you have to do things in a certain way. Most thought leaders are unconventional and are not afraid to be so. They're not scared to do things differently, outside of norm, at the risk of being criticized. Because if their unconventional ideas impact others in a positive way, it will be worth it.

Trust yourself and don't be afraid to be unconventional. It's the best way to be truly you, and that is what the world most needs—it's the greatest thing you have to offer.

**UN** ARE YOU READY TO BE
UNMESSABLE?

# TAKING A STAND

> "When you believe in a thing, believe in it all the way, implicitly and unquestionably."
>
> — Walt Disney

People want to be inspired. In the last chapter, I encouraged you to embrace different as normal. That's the big step that will allow you to lead and inspire others into action.

It's one thing to embrace and personally accept your unique point of view and methods. Putting them into practice *out there* in the real world is quite another.

How do you develop a stand that will impact others for the long term? That's the question this chapter will examine.

Walt Disney's quote above has served me well my entire life as a mantra, and especially more recently as I've developed the unapologetic brand.

Before I used "unapologetic," I used "unforgettable" in a lot of my branding. I chose that word based on what people said they wanted. "I want to be remembered" is a common request I hear from people I speak with.

Shortly after I started using unforgettable, I remembered something I had learned in Teachers College about the cognitive domain of learning, which studies the brain's cognitive functions as they relate to learning.

## THE COGNITIVE DOMAIN OF LEARNING

In 1965, a group of researchers led by Benjamin Bloom proposed that *knowledge* or *remembering* is at the lowest level of the brain's cognitive function. In other words, you may have a talk or presentation that is filled with all sorts of great information and you may be on-purpose and love your topic; however, when you present to be remembered, you've barely scratched the surface of the thinking part of the brain.

Understanding is the second level of the cognitive function of the brain. Remembering information doesn't guarantee comprehension. The next essential component of an effective talk or presentation is to provide the means for your information to be understood. This includes creating opportunities for taking notes, storytelling, demonstrations, visuals—you get the picture. When you shift the focus from delivery to comprehension, the way you speak changes. You become more descriptive, you share less (content) in a richer way, and you increase your connection with the audience. That's a good thing.

Think back to your days as a student. How much of the content that you crammed for on that big test do you actually still understand (or even remember)? Nowadays, we don't even really need to remember; we have Google acting as our *cloud brain*.

Applying is the third level. Simply, you want to allow your audience to practice. Even in a keynote presentation or a TED Talk, you can find ways to allow your audience to apply what you're talking about. Silence is your friend! Use callback, sharing, or even allow for time to "imagine yourself in this situation" and you paint a picture where your audience members can visualize and mentally walk themselves through a scenario that you create for them to apply to their own lives. The key "look for" here is that the learner applies the knowledge in context to his or her own business/life/situation.

Analyzing is the fourth level. Break down, compare, contrast, differentiate, infer, relate, and select. These are the kinds of things you want to ask to encourage analysis and this higher level of cognitive engagement. One of the best ways to achieve this is to ask the audience to run a test and look at the results (in a workshop situation). In a keynote situation, *you* run the test. Show examples from which the audience members can infer their own analyses. Design visuals and demonstrations where your point becomes obvious through observation (without you having to say it first).

Evaluating is the fifth level. After analyzing the results of a test, the next step is to evaluate. (Uh, oh...you hate tests, right? And how are you going to test an audience?) The key is to "*show* them how." Show your audience *how* to critique, summarize, conclude, and interpret the results you've led them to. Allow your audience the opportunity to evaluate equals sales! It's those speakers and leaders who incessantly do all the thinking for their audiences that have (very) limited success in converting audiences (whether it be for sales or followers). When you allow your audience to evaluate, you will also get yourself closer to claiming the throne as the leader in your field because you'll be providing a value that is not currently the norm.

Creating is the highest level of the cognitive domain. Encourage forward thinking and innovation with the concepts you speak about and the ideas and beliefs you lead with every step of the way. Encourage your audience and followers to use your fundamental beliefs to create personal success. Shift the focus from you to them. "Give" or "gift" them the ideas you share. Invite them to make those ideas their own.

## THE CONTENT EPIDEMIC

We are currently experiencing an epidemic—a content epidemic.

We are encouraged to put out content to prove our value. (We'll cover *value* in an upcoming chapter, and I'll share why you should stop delivering value and what you should deliver instead!)

The more content you create, the more you will position yourself as an authority, according to the gurus. This logic, however, seems to defy historic trends, and it completely ignores what we already know about how the brain works, as illustrated in the cognitive domain of learning.

Consider the most successful people you know. Do they produce content, or do they share what they believe? What attracts you to them?

As Simon Sinek teaches, "People don't buy what you do; they buy into why you do it."

I realized in my "unforgettable" branding that I was not actually reaching my audience beyond the first or second levels of their brain function.

One day, at a networking event, a woman approached me and asked, "What do you do?"

I am pretty much against having a stock (overly rehearsed) answer in a networking situation. What came out of my mouth was, "I empower speakers and leaders to deliver their messages and to inspire others unapologetically."

Her eyes lit up and she said, "I want that." We continued to chat for a few more minutes about how she felt ready to share what she believed in a more impactful way with her followers and the world in general.

A few days later, I received an email from her in which she expressed how our brief conversation had inspired and challenged her, and how specifically, the "unapologetic" moved her into action.

On the other hand, I also had people tell me using the word unapologetic would be too aggressive and a mistake. One person went so far as to say I would be committing *brand suicide*.

As you can see (based on this book), I counted the naysayers as positive feedback. I was causing a reaction and being remembered, so it didn't matter whether it was positive or negative.

I took a stand and made it known. I am an unapologetic speaker and coach, and I want you to deliver your message and to lead unapologetically!

Every person I met was moved by the word. Today there are over forty more "un" words and now "in" words included in the brand.

The most common question I'm asked outside of speaking, confidence, and leadership is, "How did you develop your brand? It's so strong."

Partly, I got lucky because it wasn't that I engineered it, at least not to start. It was something I said while I was just being me. "What if you're unapologetic in who you are and what you say?"

You probably wouldn't expect someone who works with speakers, performers, presenters, and leaders to say, "People don't hear what you're saying; they hear and take action on who you are being."

I was *being unapologetic.* It worked. In other words, I was embodying my message to a degree that caused other people to feel me.

Because I want to be practical so you can also *get lucky* and nail your brand, I'll share with you how I went from saying a word that seemed to polarize to creating a movement and a brand that is becoming more and more recognized.

## BIRTHING A BRAND (BY TAKING A STAND)

It really is simple. What do you take a stand for? What do you take a stand against? When you can answer these questions, you can begin to lay the foundation for the singular idea upon which you can build everything—a speaking platform, a business, a book, multiple talks, products, programs—anything becomes possible when you declare your stand.

How do you figure out your stand?

Go back to your *Everyday Extraordinary Storytelling Book* that you started in Chapter 1. If you haven't started yet, it's not too late. Start now, and remember, this is a life practice, so keep adding to your list of incidents. Not only does recording your stories serve to expose who you are, but it becomes a collection of stories for you to use in future talks, in the next book you're going to write, in stories you'll tell to inspire others and frame ideas at the next meeting you lead, and so on.

For each incident and story you document, ask yourself these questions:

1. How did I react or respond in that situation?
2. What did I make it mean?

Let's take an even deeper dive to discover (uncover) who you really are. For each incident and story, also ask yourself:

3. Who was I being?
4. So what? What do I want them to do about it?

By looking at your stories, you will uncover the lens through which you see and experience the world. Through that lens, you will discover and begin to develop your stand.

After applying the above four questions to all your past stories and incidents, take a look at the bigger picture. Notice if there are any consistencies across the timeline of your life. Notice if you react/respond a certain way throughout life.

# TAKING A STAND

Disclaimer: It's a red flag that you are resisting the process if you say, "I'm a completely different person today than I was [as a child, teen, five years ago]. After working with thousands of people, this process has worked every time. Without fail, *if* you are willing to consider the simple fact that you arrived a certain way, and that *way* is part of your being, your genetic code, this process exposes it.

Now, answer these two questions:

What do you say "Hell No" to? (What will you not stand for? What are you against? What pisses you off?)

_____

_____

_____

What do you say "Hell Yes" to? (What do you stand for? What do you believe? What fires you up?)

_____

_____

_____

What patterns are emerging? (What common thread can you identify throughout your life, including in terms of what you believe and what you take a stand for or against?)

_____

_____

_____

_____

## WHO YOU ARE BEING, MATTERS

As I've said, the reason I have anyone I work with, from individual to corporation, begin an *Everyday Extraordinary Storytelling Book* as a first step is that it exposes who you are. In your stories about your life, you show up a certain way. Taking a look at the way you show up (react/respond) will reveal your stand. Your stance (what you stand for and against) is inextricably linked to your story.

People get pretty irritated with me when I tell them, "Nobody cares about your story." I mean it. Stories are great; in fact, I believe they are essential for our survival and the advancement of society. Stories, however, do not inspire others into action unless they are aligned with a belief that leads to a lesson or a call to action.

The reason my unapologetic brand is thriving and spreading is because it is the external expression of who I am.

I'm Canadian. Everyone knows Canadians love to apologize, for everything—even if it's not our fault!

I've also lived most of my life apologizing for who I am, playing small, and being the man behind the curtain. I've even been told I'm like the Quincy Jones of speakers and leaders. As a record producer, Quincy was brilliant, and rarely in the spotlight except for awards shows or media appearances.

The fact that I've been *apologetic* my whole life fuels my unapologetic brand. I'm tired of apologizing, playing small, and being behind the curtain. I say *hell no to* apologizing for what I believe. I say *hell no* to you wasting another second playing small, or apologizing for who you are or what you believe. I say a *hell no* to you not living out your miracle because I know how that feels.

Every message, every talk, the way I work with people, my events, international experiences, masterminds, and programs—everything revolves around the idea of being unapologetic. It works because it's part of who I am and what I believe, deeply.

# TAKING A STAND

What do you believe, deeply? *That* is who you are! *That* informs your *why*. When you start speaking and leading from what you believe, even if it's not in alignment with popular opinion, you will begin to build a platform for yourself. The trick is to speak out long enough to be seen and heard and to remain unapologetic in your belief.

As I write this book, it's no surprise to me that Elon Musk launched a Tesla car into outer space or that Donald Trump is the President of the United States.

Why am I not surprised? Because both believed in what they were up to and what they had to say, unapologetically. Whether what they said was positive or not, whether you agreed with them or not is irrelevant. The fact is they are leading others by speaking (and acting) their truth while you and I purchase the next program to teach us how to *crush* social media or sell more online.

A brand (e.g., unapologetic, Elon Musk, Tesla and SpaceX, Donald Trump, Disney, Apple, and so many others) invites people to remember, understand, apply, analyze, evaluate, and finally create for themselves (think for themselves). Brands that effectively put the ball in the receiver's court and treat you like an ambassador are often the most successful.

Brands like Apple's "Think Different" and Harley Davidson's "Freedom on the Open Road" have declared what they believe (their stance) and look at their clients as ambassadors rather than transactional clients. They hand us the brand, essentially, so that we feel ownership; we feel like we are a part of something bigger, and we tell everyone!

Personal brands, speakers, and leaders have the same opportunity available to them. My brand is about *you* being unapologetic. Of course, as the creator, I will show you what it looks like to be unapologetic for me, and I will inspire you to develop your own unapologetic platform. Apple doesn't tell you how to think—it simply suggests you think differently. The rest is up to interpretation, and the products Apple sells facilitate your ability to think differently.

It all begins with deep discovery (*The Everyday Extraordinary Storytelling Book*) and declaring your stance.

I would be lying if I told you you'll nail your stance the very first time. The real secret is: Don't try to figure this out at your desk, or to intellectualize your way through this. Speak about it! Share your ideas with everyone you meet. Share your ideas with your friends, colleagues, strangers you meet at networking events, your Uber and Lyft drivers…. Tell everyone, notice how people respond and react to you, and keep experimenting. The faster you start speaking about what you believe, and the more people you tell, the faster you'll fail forward (failure is a step forward because you eliminate what doesn't work and get closer to what does) until you refine and revise to your own *unapologetic* expression of who you are.

What do you believe? (Brainstorm a few ideas/phrases that identify your stance.)

_____

_____

_____

_____

Why should someone else believe what you believe? (What's in it for them?)

_____

_____

_____

_____

_____

# TAKING A STAND

Complete this statement: Because I believe _____

_____

_____ I want you to _____

_____

(This statement often helps to clarify your stance.)

Who do you need to be in order to share this message with the world?

_____

_____

_____

Where will you share this message? (An upcoming networking event, your next talk, in a Facebook Live Stream…)

_____

_____

_____

By what date will you start sharing this message?

_____

What are you celebrating right now?

_____

_____

_____

# SPOTLIGHT: UNAPOLOGETIC INFLUENCER

## UNMESSABLE
### BY CASEY NICOLE FOX

*Casey Nicole Fox is a speaker, coach, podcaster, and author. You can learn more about her at CaseyNicoleFox.com.*

Unmessable means having a mentor and a team around you so that no matter what life throws at you, no mess will get you down. The world tells us we need to apologize for needing other people, but the reality is we actually need other people to get us out of our messes in life. And when we're in a mess, we need to embrace it so we can find those mentors and that team to help us become unmessable.

Were you ever in a food fight as a kid? Life is like a never-ending food fight in a cafeteria in an overcrowded middle school. These smelly little middle school students are throwing their only form of currency—food—at one another in a room with too many children and not enough responsibility. Some of those kids will risk it all to prove themselves, and they don't care how messy they get. Some will hide under the tables and wait until the fight is over, too afraid to stand up and do anything. Some kids will walk out of the cafeteria and go their own way, and no one will see them again. Bullies in the back corner may be rubbing some kid's face in a soggy sandwich. Everyone throwing food will be grabbing all the supplies possible in the hope to be the best and get attention. Everyone will have his or her own reasons for participating.

When I was twenty, I was in my own version of a bad food fight. I had moved to a state where I had no support system, I had no knowledge on how to "adult," and I had no financial literacy. I was like a middle schooler trying to grab as many of the resources around me as I could to prove to the world that I could do it on my own. I got four day jobs trying to pay my bills, pay off the credit cards I maxed out, and pay the day loans I got. I was lost, but my cafeteria days didn't start there.

I grew up very poor; we were evicted from every place we ever lived. I grew up with food stamps, the electricity shut off, and government aid. By age ten, I had been physically, sexually, and emotionally abused by multiple people, been in foster care and a mental institution, and tried to kill myself for the first time. My childhood "cafeteria food fight" made me react like a lot of the kids acting out to get attention. I thought the only way I could win the fight was to do it all myself.

There is one part of a food fight no one thinks about when in the middle of it: If you had help, if you had a team, you would go way further than just every-person-for-himself. It wasn't until I met my mentors when I was twenty that I started to be on the winning team of my cafeteria food-fight life.

In just three years, my mentors helped me go from four day jobs to having four businesses of my own and being president of a corporate empire bringing in a revenue of eight figures annually.

It was far from easy learning how to change my mindset to go from hiding under the table from life to knowing my strengths and joining the fight to success. No matter what we do in life, there will always be messes. You can be unmessable, though, like I am now. What that means is: When you have a support system—a coach, a mentor, a team—you become unmessable because there isn't a mess out there that will take you down. You become unmessable when you understand that in order to have massive success, you cannot do it alone; you need a team on your side to get through this cafeteria food-fight life. Now go find your mentors and your tribe and say it with me, "I *am* unmessable!"

# UN ARE YOU READY TO BE UNCORKED?

# STORYTELLING 11

"The best teacher is very interactive."

— Bill Gates

Having a strong stance, as we learned in the last chapter, becomes the foundation upon which you can build a speaking or leadership platform, and a business. Your stance will also become the lens you filter everything through—and I mean everything.

That is not to say you will lock yourself in or get typecast as a one-trick pony. Becoming known for what you believe, and having everything you say, do, promote, and sell be attached to your belief in some way strengthens your own personal brand (and increases your influence and authority in your space).

Of course, in order to bring a stance to life, you need more material. Story is undoubtedly the best way to deliver your vision to the world. In this chapter, we'll break down the common story mistakes and how to develop your stance and story in a way that will move people into inspired and long-lived action.

We are experiencing an epidemic (yes, in addition to the content epidemic). It's an epidemic of (mostly bad) storytelling.

I may as well share my unapologetic truths about *story* up front:

1. Nobody cares about your story.
2. Sharing your deepest, darkest story is often not the best choice.
3. It's highly unlikely I will become the ambassador of your story—it's yours, after all.

I said it! Nobody really cares about your story, and I really mean it. The problem (and reality) is that we are all too concerned about ourselves (yes, even you who is on a mission to save the planet and act out of service for others).

I would be untrue to my own belief system if I said otherwise.

As I said, I do believe that story is an excellent device; however, too often the story overshadows your bigger vision and mission, and causes the opposite effect you intend. In other words, used incorrectly, story can cause your audience to do nothing.

It's very easy to alienate an audience with a personal story unless you are crystal clear on the story's purpose. Whether you decide to put a story into a talk, use it to demonstrate an example, or share it to inspire others, it's critical to ask yourself, "What's the point of this story?" before you commit to including it.

Let me explain a little further. It might be appropriate, for instance, to share your story in thirty seconds or less. Your audience, if you craft the story with the end in mind (the purpose, the aha, the call to action) will get the point.

Here's what a story is not: the play-by-play retelling of, for example, your life history. These painful, seemingly never-ending stories can be identified when you hear the speaker overusing the phrases "and then...", "so what happened is...", and my personal favorites: "fast forward" and "rewind."

I'm sure you've experienced the never-ending story. It's a painful observation I made when I immigrated to the United States and attended my first conferences.

# STORYTELLING

In what I like to call the California-Nevada Triangle, which includes San Diego, Los Angeles, and Las Vegas (equally as scary as the Bermuda Triangle since speakers are sucked in and apparently put under a trance to tell terrible stories), there is no shortage of opportunity to attend a conference, event, or workshop every day of the week. Recently, an attendee of my monthly evening event, "Becoming a Paid Speaker," shared with me that she had challenged herself to attend an event or workshop every day for fourteen days straight. In Morgan's own words, "I ended up doing fifteen in a row, and it was terrible!"

My own experience of events, even the larger three-day ordeals, is that you become a victim subjected to hour upon hour of content and sales pitches. Sales pitches are always preceded by stories, and they are usually doozies! These are stories about losing it all, tragedy, being in debt for no less than $50,000, addictions, loss of friends or family—I've even heard one guru include all of these elements in the same pre-sales pitch story.

I've talked to hundreds of people about this specific phenomenon. Even those who decide to take the bait and sign up (I have, too), question the purpose of the story itself. In fact, I haven't yet come across anyone who decided to invest solely and specifically based on the story alone.

Yes, story can make you more relatable and likeable, and that's a good thing. The reality is that the story itself is rarely the point. Your story must answer the question, "What do I want them to do about it?" if it stands a chance at moving your audience into action.

Those *deepest, darkest* stories are strategically placed and used to manipulate your emotions. Sadly, some unscrupulous practitioners of neuro-linguistic programming (NLP) actually teach how to manipulate an audience for your benefit. Certainly not the intention of NLP.

You may have also experienced events where the guru shares his or her story and then plays a tear-jerking video clip. One favorite moment I've witnessed firsthand (in other words, one of the most deplorable manipulations I've ever seen implemented) is the guru who shared his story of loss and reinforced it with the opening sequence of the movie *Up*, which ends with the wife passing away before her husband gets to take her on the trip of a lifetime he had promised her—the overall point is to seed the idea to "Take action now before it's too late." Right on cue, just after the clip ended, the guru asked, "What are you waiting for? Soon it's going to be too late." Then hundreds of teary-eyed audience members rushed to the back of the room to put their deposits down on a program priced at what it would take to invest in a condo in Mexico.

Some may celebrate this as storytelling at its finest. I am making it my life's work to put an end to it, or at least turn the tide so that we have more speakers, leaders, gurus, and teachers who use stories for good.

It's clear that stories are powerful; however, in isolation, the story itself is not what will build your authority, credibility, or business. As I said earlier, I cannot become the ambassador of your story. That would require me to give up my own beliefs and just retell your story as my own. It just doesn't work.

Take a look at network marketing. Often, the most successful network marketers are the ones who attach a personal story to the product or service they represent. The representative selling beauty products because of the business opportunity will fall short of the representative who felt more confident and attracted the perfect partner after using the products herself.

Stories sell, it's true, but only when you understand the role of the story in the bigger picture.

Stories act like a bridge. They bridge the gap between me (the speaker/leader), we (the audience in front of you), and them (the people connected to your audience). When you develop your story as a bridge, you tell it differently. You weave in lessons and opportunities for the audience members to come to their own conclusions. You open the door for them to think for themselves. You encourage the audience to come up with their own conclusions. You embed your stance in the story and invite people to become ambassadors of the ideas you have, rather than your personal details. These stories are powerful, memorable, and inspiring for audiences.

## CRAFTING YOUR STORY

While this book is not meant to serve as a manual to create your talk, I would be remiss if I didn't give you actionable steps to get you started on the process of sharing your story so you can become the visionary speaker and leader I know you are.

The first step is to start by reverse-engineering your story—starting with the end in mind.

A lot of gurus out there are selling the idea that the talk outline they've created is a surefire success model.

I am unapologetically advising you that believing there is a formula for a talk will have you wasting a lot of time and even more money in pursuit of something that does not exist.

In fact, the world-famous TED organization warns against coaches who try to sell formulas and perfect talk structures. They believe, as do I, that the best talks are structured in three parts (or three acts, if you will): a beginning, a middle, and an end.

Of course, as you grow in experience and confidence, your three-act structure will evolve. For instance, my talks often include an overture (leading up to the first act) and a double ending (or an encore). Still, the overall talk will fall into three big picture parts.

Hint: Your third act (the ending) will always be some sort of call to action. Whether it will be a physical call to action, an invitation to think differently, or the insinuation that there is something more to explore, every time you speak, you must have a call to action (the point).

Before you start writing out your ideas for your three-act talk, consider sketching out concepts and ideas for it.

## FROM WHO TO HOW TO WOW

One of the big mistakes people make when beginning to craft a story or a talk is starting with the question, "What should I talk about?" Instead, start with *who*.

## DEFINE THE WHO

*Who* is you. You are the critical piece—the piece that, most often, fails to show up (unapologetically and in your full glory).

In other words, *who* are you? Who are you showing up as for your audience? What is your stand? What do you believe in? And most importantly:

*Who* will you *be* to give an audience a reason to reject you so they can accept you?

When you are clear on who you are, and why you are who you are, those who experience you will take note.

Understanding who you are must come before you even tackle your *why*, as I discussed earlier.

Can you see how critical who *you* are is as it relates to the why? In order to have a why that is in alignment (and will impact others), it's absolutely imperative that you understand who you are (all of you—good, bad, and ugly).

*Who* is also the "big picture" view of your audience. When you know *who* your audience is, you can design the way you deliver your *why*—the purpose for your talk or presentation and the desired final result.

The *why* for a group of beginners reflects their needs directly, which would be different than the *why* for a group of seasoned experts in any given field.

Continue to explore your *who* based on where your audience is at in its understanding of your idea, belief, or the given topic you're presenting.

Yes, here's where you have to commit to truly understanding your audience and its needs/wants. Ask yourself:

- What do they know?
- What do they not know?
- What do they need to know (to achieve your *why*)?

## IDENTIFY YOUR WHY

Before you stop reading and judge me for sharing something you probably already know, stick with me because there is more to *why* than you may realize.

*Why* is the desired result.

Why are you speaking, presenting, or leading, and *why* should someone listen to, learn from, follow, or invest in you?

You see, when you look at the learning process (also applicable to the sales process), the end result is the point. Take a cookbook or an online recipe as the example. The first thing you are presented with is the finished product: the recipe title and often a picture. The *why*, uncluttered.

Imagine, instead, if you were presented with blank ingredient lists and instructions, and the final product was left to be a mystery, because you, the author of the recipe, wanted someone to "learn by doing" and achieve an Emeril Lagasse-like "BAM" only in the final moments, because "That is impactful."

Your *why* needs to be clearly defined, and everything you say and do must lead the audience to the *why*.

Now, here's the fine detail that will make a big difference. *You* must be intrinsically and inextricably connected to the *why*. You represent the why.

In an instructional design model (my teaching background has served me well when working with speakers and leaders), the *why* is referred to as the enduring understanding (big words, big concept, easier to digest than you think). "Enduring" refers to the big ideas you want people to truly "get inside of" or internalize even after they've forgotten the finer details.

So then, your *why* also keeps you on track and helps to distinguish between:

- Information worth being familiar with
- Information/actions important to know and do
- Enduring understandings

A warning. Diving into developing content before you have a fully developed *why* (that isn't attached to who you are) is a recipe for a disaster (which I see far too often).

*Who* you are and *why* you are not only anchor your entire talk and platform, but they drive your audience forward—closer to your vision, mission, and purpose—and inspire them into *action!*

## DEFINE YOUR *WHERE* AND *WHAT*

*Where* are you meeting your audience? What do they already know?

*Where* are you taking your audience? (What's the transformation you facilitate?)

*What:* The acceptable evidence that will validate and prove that you've moved your audience from the starting point to the desired destination/outcome.

You thought *this* was the content part, right? And it is, sort of.

How will you measure results, success, or progress?

This question raises a lot of questions about logistics, so I'm here to challenge you to get crystal clear on this step because it is one of the most important things to consider if you want to achieve lasting influence.

What is *What*?

Here are some success-measuring tools to consider:

- Conversion/Metrics (in a funnel or sales situation)
- Observation (in a live setting)
- Dialogue/Discussion
- Quizzes/Tests
- Prompts/Agreement (especially in sales and transformation)
- Performance Tasks
- Self-Assessments

If you deliver a content-heavy presentation, provide opportunities to use content in context. Show how what you speak about can be applied to the person (every single one of them) sitting in the audience (*who*).

Include prompts and provide opportunities to share to confirm agreement and understanding.

Take polls. Make observations. If you're speaking about living a life on fire, for example, and you observe the audience is not "being" on fire when you ask for agreement, there is a disconnect. While people may be hearing what you say, you are not creating an experience that will transform them. So challenge them to respond in a way that lets them feel what it is to live a life on fire!

*Why?* Because that is what you believe and what you want for every member of the audience.

*Who?* Because that is who you *are*, and whom you know every member of your audience to be (their true potential).

It's critical that you do not measure results only at the end. By then, it's too late.

Ask yourself, "*What* tools, devices, and opportunities, *over time* (over the entire talk; good things take time, and repetition) will I put in place to determine that my outcome is being achieved?" Stay true and committed to your *why* and *who* and actively define the *what* throughout.

## PLAN YOUR *HOW*

Now, you're just about ready to create your actual talk or presentation. Before we deal with the *how*, we have some business to finish with *what*. (I know, this is the hardest part—to resist planning *how* to present until the last moment! Stick with me; the results will astound you.)

Determine *what* is needed for success (Yes, the content!)

- *What* knowledge/skills are required to achieve the goal/desired results?

- *What* activities/experiences will best teach/deliver/instill those skills/knowledge?

- *What* resources, materials, or platforms are the best to accomplish the desired goal?

# STORYTELLING

(It's important to note that I included content under the *how*. *How* you deliver content is as critical as *what* you choose to deliver. They are linked.)

*How* will you deliver so you can most effectively connect your audience to the *why*?

- Will you use personal stories or stories from others?
- Will you use effective slides and language to build desire and encourage transformation?
- Will you present for thirty minutes, one hour, or three days?
- Will you leverage your own content or use curated content?

Now is when you get to make the slides, write the copy, and design the flow of your presentation, always with the *why*, *who*, and *what* in mind.

The moment will come when your *why* becomes the *why* of those in your audience because you have taken the time to understand them, speak to them directly, and include the measure for results that allows them to internalize/see personal value in what you offer (be it education, transformation, or further pursuit).

The *single biggest* mistake speakers make—even successful speakers—is to jump into content selection and design too quickly. Even those speakers who can quickly and eloquently express their *why* make this mistake.

Look, just because you know your *why* and can recite it doesn't mean you've infused your talk with it. When in doubt, ask yourself, "*Why* am I including this?" "*Why* does it matter?" "*Why* am I doing it this way?" and "*Who* am I?" "*Who* am I being for my audience?" "*Who* do I want my audience to be?" When the answers to those questions directly link back to your actual *why* and *who* you are, then you know you are on the path to creating a transformative experience for your audience.

## BEYOND BEYONCÉ

Read the opening lyrics to the Beyoncé hit, "Single Ladies (Put a Ring on It)." They illustrate a fundamental understanding about engagement (not the marriage kind) that has allowed the star to rise to the level of success and fame she enjoys today.

She and the writing team behind the song—Terius "The-Dream" Nash, Thaddis "Kuk" Harrell, and Christopher "Tricky" Stewart—understand one simple concept that has stood the test of time when it comes to impact, influence, and virality.

Repetition.

Without getting into a very deep discussion of it (I could write an entire book on this idea alone), repetition has, throughout the ages, been one of the single most effective ways to enroll people, sell, create impact, celebrate, remember, and honor others.

We love repetition.

And yet, in the speaking and leadership space, I often hear, "But I don't want to be too repetitive," "I already said that once. I want to keep it interesting," "We tried that once," and other similar protestations that ignore a millennia's worth of data that proves we respond to repetition.

While you probably shouldn't start leading by repeating phrases as if you're delivering Beyoncé's next hit song, remembering to use repetition as part of your platform will allow you to gain traction that simply cannot be gained in any other way.

Embrace phrases, ideas, and actions that engage your audience. Create the opportunity for them to take part in what you're up to.

Using repetition will allow you to reach your audience (past, present, and future) in a proven way that is both effective and relatively simple.

# STORYTELLING

## EVERYDAY STORYTELLING

My own personal experience with storytelling happened as an accidental discovery while I was teaching freshman music. I loved to get to know my students more personally, but it wasn't easy to do when they had clarinets or trumpets in their faces for an entire period. So I would spend a few moments during the beginning of most classes asking students to share something about their night or weekend... in other words, to tell me a story.

Almost without exception, the stories were terrible. In fact, they weren't stories at all. For example:

Me: "Who did something exciting this weekend and has a story to share?"

Student raises hand and I ask him to share.

Student: "I had family over and we ate."

Me: [waiting for more. Smiling]

Student: [Blank Stare. Smiling]

Me: "How many people did you have over? What did you eat?"

Student: "Oh, there were about twenty-seven people present. We ate homemade Indian food."

Me: "Wow! I don't think I know twenty-seven people that I want to invite for dinner at my house [trying to be funny]. Was the food good?"

Student: "It was good."

This was typical.

So, of course, I began my crusade to teach these young minds to tell better stories, and I encouraged them to be more descriptive, to reverse-engineer to a punchline or a point, to be humorous, entertaining, and inspiring where appropriate.

Here's where it gets interesting. The better at telling stories my students became, the better they became as musicians, too. As I saw this pattern emerge, I tested it. Without fail, students and whole classes that I spent a few minutes working on storytelling with (though they didn't specifically know it—they just thought my obsession with having them describe their lives outside my classroom was funny) had stronger musicianship, especially when it came to playing expressively—essentially, they were able to tell better stories in the way they played their music. They brought the music to life.

In Chapter 17, I will share how I took this whole experiment a step further and it became the foundation of the work I do around the world. It all started with my obsession for hearing good stories.

Stories, when done right, become an interactive and invitational component. Your stories are not the point; they are the bridge between you and the audience. They humanize you and allow others to consider their own stories and how they fit.

As the Bill Gates quote that opens this chapter states, great teachers are interactive. Remember, it's not your job to give your audience all the answers. It *is*, however, your job to lead them to discovering and developing their own conclusions. Speakers and leaders who understand this are the world's best. Are you ready to step onto the world stage as an interactive and engaging storyteller and leader?

What is your biggest takeaway from this chapter, and how will you implement it in your future teaching, speaking, and storytelling?

_____

_____

_____

_____

# SPOTLIGHT: UNAPOLOGETIC INFLUENCER

## UNCORKED
**BY CINDY ASHTON**

*Cindy Ashton is the CEO of Speaker Stardom, the award-winning TV host of* Cindy Uncorked, *and a singer, entertainer, keynote speaker, and elite level presentation strategist. You can learn more about her at* CindyAshton.com.

Getting uncorked is the art of expressing your thoughts with intelligence and kindness while being willing to listen to the opinions of others, without judgment. When we are able to communicate, listen, and respond from a grounded space, we are able to bridge the gap between people of different races, religions, experiences, and backgrounds.

Being unapologetic allows us to get uncorked in a way that is completely untethered, uncensored, and filled with conviction. It allows us to stand in that voice and let it carry far and wide, regardless of what others think.

I am totally fed up with people expressing their concerns about an important issue or challenge they are facing, only to have other people either:

A. Need to "one up" them by voicing their concerns as a way to discount the other person's feelings and experiences. They need to be right instead of listening and being open to entertaining a different point of view.

B. Saying "Your thoughts create your reality" and essentially shaming that person for the difficulty he or she is going through. Um, since when has being human meant that everything will be roses all the time? This response is so unbelievably uncompassionate.

C. Trying to "fix" the problem without asking if the person is open to advice or without fully understanding the situation.

All these responses shut down people's ability to be truly uncorked and express their deepest truths. Being unapologetically uncorked is being able to have a voice without fear of other people's responses.

How do you become uncorked? First off, breathe. I mean it. Breathe. The majority of people live in an overstimulated, hyper state, so they are unaware of their triggers and get stuck in their egos. Imagine what the world would be like if we could slow down. Take a breath in and exhale out, nice and long, several times. Deep breathing will stimulate the parasympathetic nervous system, which calms the heart rate, relaxes the muscles, and focuses the mind.

In a grounded state, we are able to get uncorked from our truth and not our fears. And we are able to drop our defenses, really listen, and respond to other people with kindness and intelligence.

Let me share an example by telling a story of how I live uncorked. I have always been daring in my thinking, seeking truth, and fighting for the underdog. But most of my life, I was punished for being me. Punished for standing out and being different. Shamed if I were too vocal.

My earliest memory of speaking my mind and not backing down was in the eleventh grade in social studies class. I gave a well-researched, hour-long presentation on why I believed prostitution should be legalized. I showed evidence of how so many innocent women and some men end up being sex slaves, and how motorcycle gangs were profiting and committing crimes from it. I shared how controlling prostitution would cut down on crimes, help the victims, reduce abuse, and clean up crime.

I had thirty classmates tearing me apart the entire hour because, apparently, I was immoral and a sinner. I stood my ground despite all the hate. And I was proud of myself. I was truly uncorked!

More recently, I produced my TV show, *Cindy Uncorked*. The first topic we tackled out of the gate was how trauma sits in women's vaginas and causes them depression, anxiety, and all kinds of medical issues. I got uncorked about something that made people feel uncomfortable. I had hundreds of women and a few men email me personally to tell me how that episode gave them a voice in a society that shames people for having problems. They told me it gave them insight into why they had had so many miscarriages, painful sex, endometriosis, and other issues. It gave light to their suffering...and now they have a path to heal.

I also got tons of hate mail and even one death threat, claiming that I am a sinner for talking about "such things."

Thanks to me being bold enough to produce a TV show that tackles provocative topics, I got an amazing opportunity—a TV contract with an alternative lifestyle network, e360tv, which now has me on 186 million screens worldwide. Since then, my career has been rising. I am gracing red carpets, including the Oscars, and mostly, making a huge impact by being uncorked!

It's time for you to become uncorked too. I know the thought of it can be scary, but on the other side of fear, squashing your voice, and having to be right lies freedom. Stepping out and sharing your deepest truths, while being okay that others may not agree, opens you up to building a community of people who will love and adore you for you. Being uncorked will release you from getting in conflict and, instead, allow you to understand the world in a more holistic way. It will give you an opportunity to serve yourself and more people in a deeply satisfying way.

I spent most of my life vacillating between being uncorked and then shutting up because I wanted to be loved and accepted. I felt like I was suffocating. I was at war with the person I knew I was and the person who was falsely presenting herself to the world. It was a nightmare. If I hadn't learned how to stand in my own power of being uncorked, I would still be suffocating. And I wouldn't be reaching millions as I am now and having an impact.

So get uncorked. You know it's time. I guarantee you'll be amazed by the transformation you'll experience!

**UN** ARE YOU READY TO BE
UNWAVERING?

# HAVING FAITH

## 12

"Most brands started from a strong base and kept a strong belief."

— Daymond John

Someone is waiting for you. Yes, you.

*She* isn't waiting for you to deliver value or content; *she* is waiting for you to show up being authentic and vulnerable and willing to share the stories that create connection, community, collaboration, and positive transformation. As you learned in the last chapter, stories are powerful. A fine line is also often crossed when it comes to storytelling. Reverse-engineering your story to be the bridge between you and the rest of the world will keep you on track to building your platform and brand inclusively, with integrity, and in a way that will build your positive influence.

As you share yourself with the world, people will begin to experience who you are. They will form beliefs based on what you believe and how you share what you believe with the world. These perceptions co-mingle with your own beliefs to create your brand.

Development isn't always fun. This chapter covers perhaps the most challenging aspect of becoming a visionary speaker and leader: having faith.

Why does faith belong in a section on developing into a speaker and leader? Just like the *letting go* muscle, having faith is something that needs to be practiced, often.

Also, I've come to observe a counterintuitive phenomenon. The more you believe in yourself and, as a result, have that same belief for others, the more people will, in turn, believe in, support, and celebrate you.

Faith goes against our pre-programmed intuition for personal survival. Our obsession with ourselves has been exponentially magnified with the advent of selfie-hungry social media platforms. Even the famed Facebook algorithm is self-obsessed, seemingly favoring images with smiling selfies more than any other kind of image.

The problem, just like with fear and comparanoia, is this: Developing a personal brand and a message with which you intend to transform your slice of the world comes with a lot of roadblocks in many different forms. Your *faith* or *believing* muscle needs to be strong when you are the messenger *and* the message because you will be tested every step of the way.

As a speaker and leader, you use words and your way of being to influence and inspire your audiences into action. Even more powerful is what lies beneath the words and your intent—your beliefs.

## THE POWER OF YOU

On Saturday morning, June 4, 2011, I was at home sitting in bed, catching up on the world news on my laptop. My dog, Galileo, was snuggled beside me.

It was the first Saturday off I'd had in months. Between teaching and the yoga studio, life was busy. You already know the outcome of the yoga studio—by September of that year, it would go bankrupt. What I didn't tell you about yet was the *main* event, if you will, that would be one of the biggest tests of faith I ever had.

# HAVING FAITH

It was a rainy morning. Stormy, in fact. By some stroke of luck (you'll understand why shortly), this was the first year I had decided, along with my teaching partner at school, not to be involved in the local street festival, a major event that always brought the town together. We would do performances, have a booth, create surprise flash mobs—it was an all-day affair that would start before sunrise and end well into the evening.

This Saturday, I was home and thankful for a quiet morning.

It was a wicked storm. At 10:38:49 a.m. (yes, I'd come to learn the exact moment after the fact), I heard a very loud bang. It sounded like lightning and thunder at the same time. I didn't pay much attention at first, except I noticed my laptop seemed to have frozen up.

Ten days prior, I had rented out a room in my house to a firefighter. He was not supposed to be home either, but suddenly, I heard him run down the stairs and out the front door. I thought to myself, "That's odd.... I didn't even know he was home."

Seconds later, he came back in and yelled up the stairs, "Hey, Davide, do you have a fire extinguisher?" I thought maybe he had burnt toast or something. Then he said, "And where's your ladder...and attic access?"

I instantly jumped out of bed and opened my bedroom door. I set the stepladder in my bedroom closet (where the attic access panel was located) and pointed him in its direction.

Picture this: a 6' 4" man holding a portable fire extinguisher that looked to be the size of his thumb standing on a three-step stepladder, and yes, he was the image of the stereotypical annual firefighters' calendar's cover model. It was actually a very comical scene.

He popped his head up into the attic and then crouched down, extinguisher still in hand, ready to activate, and said, "Call 911!"

When I started to ask a question, he quickly interrupted me and said, "Don't ask questions! Call 911, and we've got to get your car out of the garage!"

I called 911 and reported, "My roof is on fire."

I grabbed Galileo and ran down the stairs. By the time we were crossing the front door's threshold, I could smell the smoke.

I put Galileo in the car, took the car out of the garage, and parked it on the street. Then my firefighter roommate and I carried my Vespa scooter out of the garage onto the sidewalk. I remember he said, "We don't want to leave anything with fuel in the garage."

After what felt like an eternity, a fire truck arrived. Then another, and another, and a fourth one, too.

By this point, I was standing across the street on the neighbors' covered porch. Maybe I was in shock, but in my mind, I couldn't understand what all the fuss was about. And then I saw them cutting the roof open with a chainsaw.

I distinctly remember taking photos every couple of minutes as the action unfolded. Still, in my mind, everything was going to be okay. I mean, houses don't burn down in suburbs because of storms, do they?

My firefighter roommate was standing beside me when a siren went off. It sounded like no siren I'd ever heard before. I turned to him and asked, "What does that mean?" I remember seeing the color drain from his face. He didn't turn, he didn't move, his expression didn't change, but he managed to mumble a few times, "They can't save the house.... They can't save it.... They're evacuating...."

And then, at 11:29 a.m., everything went up in thick black smoke. Every window blew out, and the twenty-seven firefighters who were working to contain the blaze stopped what they were doing and backed away from the structure.

I also remember seeing two of the firefighters run out the front door—thick black smoke still spewing from it.

Five hours later, my house was gone. Everything inside was incinerated, the floors were unstable, and the basement may as well have been a swimming pool because there was so much water in it.

By 5:00 p.m., I was alone. The Red Cross has come to offer my roommate a hotel room to stay and some essentials. All emergency crews had left, all the reporters, all the onlookers—everyone had left. It was me and a security guard sitting in his car across the street. The home was still smoldering.

I had a choice to make. I thought I'd either drown myself in the basement or just move on and call someone for help.

I couldn't stand the thought of leaving Galileo behind, so I chose to make a call. But I had no idea who to call. I didn't want to bother anyone, and more importantly, I really didn't have a lot of close friends locally.

Eventually, I decided to call my teaching partner. For some reason, I thought it would be appropriate to open with small talk. "How are you? How's your weekend?" I asked her. She started to share, "Wow, we've had *a day*! We had to bring Mom to the hospital, so we spent most of the day there and now—"

I cut her off. "Kathy, my house burned down today."

## YOU ARE A FORCE

You may be wondering how the story of my house burning down fits in a book about empowering you to be a visionary leader and speaker and what it has to do with developing your stance, your story, and your unique platform.

What I didn't tell you in the story is what I believed (and knew to be true) as I stood watching my home burn down: I had caused the fire.

Let me explain. In the fire's aftermath, my case became quite notable. It was determined that my home had been struck by 13 kilo-amps of lightning. Multiple investigators, including CSI units, wanted to see it for themselves. It's not a normal occurrence to have a total loss as a result of a lightning strike.

Experts kept telling me that the odds were outrageous. "I've never seen anything like this in over thirty years," one investigator commented.

I knew, however, that I wasn't the lucky winner of the lightning lottery. In the six months preceding that Saturday morning, because of the pressure of the failing yoga studio, I had started to feel like I was drowning. Every night before I went to bed, every morning when I woke up, and practically every waking moment, I wondered what it would be like to have a fresh start…a clean slate…to start over.

I prayed for it. I believed that somehow things would work themselves out.

Of course, I forgot to specify (here is where Lady Universe can be a capricious soul) exactly what that working out looked like, so I got exactly what I asked for: a clean sweep.

It was like a flashback to my Arctic experience. Once again, I was discovering that I was the problem and, more importantly, that my thoughts and beliefs were extremely powerful!

If I were able to get what I wanted (which was actually not what I wanted at all) based on my thoughts and beliefs, what could be possible if I focused my thoughts and beliefs on exactly what I did want?

## WHAT DO YOU WANT?

The pieces of your life's puzzle all fit together, whether you realize it or not. I've learned that patience, radical commitment, and deep belief are the key ingredients in allowing the puzzle pieces to come together as they are designed to.

After my birth family disowned me in 2009 and I redefined my definition of family, I started spending more time visiting someone I had originally met on Cayman Brac in 1997. Anita was a brilliant businesswoman who traveled the world doing continuing medical education trips for doctors who also loved to scuba dive. I was hired by the hotel her group was staying at to create and run an adventure camp experience for the diving doctors' kids.

Over the years, Anita and her husband Pete had adopted me as their own. I refer to them as Mom and Dad and visit them for the holidays and impromptu weekends. They lived in Arizona, which made San Diego just a short trip away, and I'd always been attracted to San Diego.

In 1993, when I was sixteen, I had visited San Diego on a high school band trip. A couple of days into the trip, I had declared out loud to my friends, "One day, I'm going to live here."

In 2015, I felt ready to find love. I also knew I would like to live in a warmer climate. Often, when visiting Anita and Pete, I would take road trips out to Vegas, Palm Springs, and San Diego. On this trip in particular, in 2015, I decided to change my online dating profile location to San Diego after visiting for a couple of days.

In the summer of 2015, I received a message from Heath who lived in San Diego. It was the first and only message I received since I had changed my profile to show my location as San Diego.

Today, Heath is my husband and we live together in San Diego with Galileo.

This story began in 1993 with a bold declaration. I believed that *one day* I'd live in San Diego.

Through luck or divine intervention, in 1997 I met the woman who would ultimately become surrogate family to me.

In 2015, my desire and belief in finding an amazing man to share my life with came to fruition.

All the pieces fit together, perfectly. The foundation on which the pieces rest is my belief.

## WHAT DO YOU BELIEVE IS POSSIBLE FOR YOU?

Here's one final story to show you how powerful belief is and why you need to become vulnerable enough to share what you believe with others if you truly want to lead others to discovering their own greatness.

On December 2, 2016, I attended the Life on Fire annual event, *Ignite*. On the first day, I sat down for the first time with the woman who would become my coach, Jenn. I asked her, in no uncertain terms, "If I sign up for this coaching program—and let me remind you, I'm not even a US resident yet, so I can't even work officially—will this work for me?"

Jenn stared me straight in the eyes without any hesitation and reassured me that based on my expertise and what I brought to the table, I would be able to create success with the support of her coaching program.

I signed up. I had absolutely no idea how I would make it work, but I believed, and I borrowed Jenn and Donna's belief in me. (Donna runs the operation and is one of my kindred spirits.)

On December 7, 2016, I received my green card, and I have since gone on to be one of Life on Fire's biggest success stories.

I'm not smarter, a greater expert, or luckier than anyone else. I just go all in, and I believe, obsessively. There have been too many instances in my life when I prayed and believed in what I didn't actually want. My fire really taught me to get very intentional with my thoughts and beliefs.

As a speaker, leader, coach, or mentor, not only do you have to have extreme belief in what you believe, but you also have to overflow and believe in others. I believe you are already a speaker and leader. Because I believe that, my clients succeed and, more importantly, believe in themselves and empower even more people to believe, too.

Every nation's leader believes—whether we agree with that leader's platform or not.

Every religious leader believes.

Every great speaker, performer, athlete, and company founder believes.

Daymond John believed in FUBU enough to have the audacity to practically stalk LL Cool J until he agreed to take a photo wearing a branded sweater.

Success demands belief. The development phase of a talk or a leadership platform will test you and your beliefs. Just like Walt Disney believed in Disney World, Elon Musk believed in Tesla, and Jesus believed in his vision of unconditional love, you have a lot to gain by standing firm in what you believe. The more you believe, the more you will convince others to believe in you—and themselves.

Also, it requires special mention that the most successful people are those who *also* surrender to others' beliefs when necessary.

People like Walt Disney, Elon Musk, Mother Teresa, and Oprah Winfrey never could have accomplished everything alone; they had to believe in the team of experts they built around them.

I had no idea how I'd be able to rebuild a business from scratch when I immigrated to this country, despite my previous successes. But Jenn believed in me.

I didn't know I could write a musical when I was nineteen, but my mentors, Mr. Gorman and Mr. Tos, believed in me.

As I began to write this book, I reached out to both Mr. Gorman and Mr. Tos. When I did, Brian Tos told me, "I saw a gifted, young musical talent that deserved opportunities to expand his horizon. Sean Gorman gave me the chance to assemble you and a handful of other talented youth and lead that group to what I still believe was the greatest high school musical experience I have ever been involved in."

Have a strong belief in yourself, and know when to surrender and borrow belief from those who also see and support your vision. When you do, the blessings and ripples created will grow exponentially.

What do you believe is possible for you in your business or life? Brainstorm your wildest, most audacious outcome. Be specific.

_____

_____

_____

What specifically will you need to believe over the longer term in order to bring this outcome to life?

_____

_____

_____

How can you start to program yourself to believe this? (For example, I set my phone alarm to go off five to ten times per day. Each time it goes off, I recite what I want to believe about myself.)

_____

_____

_____

What support will you need to keep you on track when your belief is challenged or questioned?

_____

_____

_____

## SPOTLIGHT: UNAPOLOGETIC INFLUENCER

# UNWAVERING
**BY NICK UNSWORTH**

*Nick Unsworth is a speaker, author, and high performance coach. You can learn more about him at LifeOnFire.com.*

When I think about being unwavering, I think about being rock solid—being rock solid in your beliefs, truth, and vision for your life. To let *nothing* get in the way of your God-given assignment for your life.

To be unapologetically unwavering is not to care what other people think about your life's purpose. When you are unapologetically unwavering, you relentlessly pursue your assignment and calling without letting anyone or anything get in the way.

When you decide to be unwavering, you are saying no to being average or mediocre, or to settling. You are committing to living out your God-given assignment, no matter what. You become the kind of person who will relentlessly pursue your purpose and assignment despite what others say or think about it.

You become the kind of person who gets excited when you hear others tell you that you can't do it.

It's a decision to think: "I can. I will. Watch me!" That is living the unwavering way.

I share with you what it means to be unwavering because I want you to realize you have a choice. You're not born an unwavering person—you *decide* to *be* an unwavering person.

So I don't care how young or old you are...my goal is for you to lock in the vision and purpose for your life and decide to be unwavering in your pursuit of it.

Let nothing stop you along the way. When people say you can't, recognize that's the point where "most" people would waver and quit their dreams.

Not you. You hear their feedback, and deep down inside, you become even more fired up and hungry to achieve it.

Be unwavering...and turn your dreams into reality now!

I know—it's easier said than done, so let me share with you how I've managed to embody being unwavering. After eleven business failures, I found myself more than $50,000 in debt at age twenty-eight. Everyone told me to quit being an entrepreneur.

"Be more like your brother," they said. "Go out and get a real job."

However, I stood in my truth and decided to be unwavering despite my fears. I learned how to leverage my fear and turn it into unwavering passion and fire to make my dreams come true.

I was determined to create a business and then go out and sell it exactly when I said I would—before my thirtieth birthday.

When you choose to live your life in an unwavering way, you are saying *yes* to your dreams.

How did I become so stubborn and determined to follow my own path? Perhaps it started when I was a freshman in high school. Up until then, I was easily influenced by my peers. Then my best friends turned on me and began to bully me.

At that point, I said, "Enough is enough.... I'm going to go out and play football, and by my senior year, be a varsity player."

I wasn't athletic. I wasn't "good enough" in the eyes of most, but I was unwavering in my decision to be a varsity player.

By my senior year, I was the starting center and middle linebacker. In fact, I even got into the High School Hall of Fame.

*Anything is possible*...when you decide to be unwavering in your dreams. Being unwavering has allowed me to achieve things that others thought were literally impossible. It has allowed me to do literally anything I put my mind to. It has allowed me to have an impact on others around the world—in fact, I've built an entire company around it. Today, I help others have unwavering faith in their vision and purpose, and now I have an army of people all over the world who are turning their dreams into reality.

I hope now I've helped you as well. Be unwavering. It's the best way to reach your full potential.

# PART III
# DELIVERING YOUR VISION

**UN** ARE YOU READY TO BE
UNQUIET?

# SPEAKING YOUR TRUTH

"Speaking your truth is the most powerful tool we all have."

— Oprah Winfrey

It's time to take action. The first two sections of this book focused on discovery and development. It's critical to understand that discovery and development take time and they are a lifelong practice. They will, however, paralyze you if you do not choose to deliver your message to the world right now. Delivering your vision based on who you are and what you believe is the focus of the next seven chapters.

What you believe matters. If you believe you aren't good enough, your audience will feel it. If you believe you are busy, you will feel it. If you believe you matter, those around you will also feel they matter. Whether it's a phenomenon similar to sympathetic vibration or it's part of the miracle of life, it works, and my wish for you is that you believe, deeply, in yourself and the work you're doing in the world.

As I illustrated in the last chapter, believing is powerful on its own. In fact, your beliefs often override the words you say. What I've found with everyone I've worked with over the last twenty-five years is that beliefs are further strengthened when you begin speaking about them.

Without exception, the biggest resistance to speaking or stepping into the spotlight I hear is some version of, "I'm not ready, yet."

Earlier, I mentioned that I wholeheartedly believe you are already a speaker—you arrived into this world as one. What exactly aren't you ready for?

Also, without exception, everyone I've ever worked with who just puts him- or herself out there and starts to speak (good, bad, or ugly) gets results.

You can spend your entire life waiting to be ready, or you can just start speaking. The thing is, when you are sitting at your desk or in your comfy chair thinking about your message, the only filter you have is you. No offense, but you're probably the worst filter for your own ideas; it's just the way it is.

Even this book, if I keep thinking about it instead of writing it and sharing it with the world, will never have the impact I believe it will have if it stays in my head.

## YOU'RE READY TO BE UNQUIET AND UNANONYMOUS

What do you believe? How often do you share it?

Who are you? How often do you share who you truly are with others?

What are you waiting for? What holds you back from sharing what you believe with the world today?

_____

_____

_____

_____

# SPEAKING YOUR TRUTH

Ellen DeGeneres spent a lot of time being quiet about who she really was. Her television show character was loved. But as Ellen evolved in her off-air life, she knew she needed to speak out and *become* more of herself.

After Ellen came out on her TV show, her co-star Joely Fisher told *Vanity Fair*, "I saw someone literally get lighter in her feel and in her vibe. She was like a caged bird.... I saw a shift in her gait; I saw a shift in the way she carried herself."

Even after the world knew, it took Ellen quite some time to be able to talk about it herself or even say the words, "I'm gay."

I can definitely relate to Ellen. Although I decided to start telling everyone I was gay in 2009, I wasn't really comfortable talking about it until a few years later. Even after getting married, living in the fairly liberal California, I noticed that I didn't immediately share freely who I was or what I believed—and that was six years later!

It takes time. If you think right away that you're going to start sharing your ideas and what you believe confidently and create the impact you imagine you'll create, you may set yourself up for disappointment.

The disappointment that comes for newer speakers and leaders when they don't experience the proverbial standing ovation and validation for their message can cause them to give up.

Imagine if Ellen, after coming out to the world (the episode alone was seen over 44 million times!) and a year later having her show cancelled, gave up because she believed people didn't want to hear her message. We would have missed out on all the comedy, joy, gratitude, and blessings she models on her extremely successful talk show today.

## YOU GIVE UP TOO SOON

Being unquiet while being authentic to yourself, your ideas, and your message for the world requires an unwavering commitment and a blind faith.

When you begin, you will not see the end in sight, at least not the outcome that will actually come to pass. Despite not knowing the exact outcome, you have to find it within yourself to stay unquiet, to continue to share your message.

And if you don't believe your message is being heard, what if instead of changing your message, you change your audience?

The interesting thing that happens when you are committed to sharing your message and ideas (no matter what) is they begin to grow, strengthen, and become even more focused.

The more you speak (even one-on-one) and the more you are in situations where you are exchanging dialogue about your ideas with others, the more your ideas will come to life.

Most people, however, don't speak intentionally or long enough about what they believe to keep themselves in the running to be the next world leader, speaker, or visionary. Will you make that same mistake?

## YOUR TRUTH. YOUR PLATFORM.

In 2018, Oprah Winfrey became the first African-American woman to accept the Cecil B. DeMille Award at the Golden Globes. She had one message for the world: Tell your story because you, too, can make a difference.

This is no secret. History has shown us the truth of it over and over again. Those who speak out and believe their truth change the world. Now it's your turn to speak your truth and harness the power of what you believe for the good of your audience that is waiting to hear from you.

# SPEAKING YOUR TRUTH

Where can you speak about and get into discussions about your ideas and what you believe? (name the networking group, location, opportunities, etc.)

_____

_____

_____

What will try to stop you from pursuing the above opportunities?

_____

_____

_____

How will you overcome the obstacles you identified above?

_____

_____

_____

# SPOTLIGHT: UNAPOLOGETIC INFLUENCER

## UNQUIET
**BY CARMENZA DAVID**

*Carmenza David connects people to your business. You can learn more about her at SanDiegoBC.com.*

For me, being unquiet means speaking my mind when it makes a positive difference for those involved. As long as my words are truthful, loving, vulnerable and kind, inquisitive, supportive, inclusive and fun, compassionate, and motivating while I'm expressing them, it means I am free to give and to receive. It means I'm honoring my true self. It means I'm holding myself high, which, in turn, will allow me to hold others in the same way.

Being unquiet means taking responsibility for my actions, asking for help, being an active member of my community, being a leader, making a difference, every day speaking in gratitude, hearing others, hearing myself, and hearing my soul.

I want others to be unquiet with their feelings, to be unquiet with their loved ones, to use unquiet in counting their blessings, and their inner gifts.

I learned to be unquiet as a child. I'm number six in a family of seven children, so being unquiet was how I dealt with life in my family. If I didn't speak, no one noticed me. From a very early age, I used my voice to be heard, to be seen, to be me.

Being unquiet is my choice and represents who I truly am. No one "should" consider being or embracing being unquiet. If you feel the urge, the need to be less silent, if you ever feel more could be said, or you want to speak from the heart but are unsure, I encourage you to try. Being unquiet is freeing, invigorating, and powerful!

Today, I admire those—such as members of the "Me, Too" movement—who now, better than ever before, are able to be unquiet and be true to themselves.

After all these years, I'm still learning how to get better at being unquiet. The year 2016 was one of complete inner transformation for me. I "experienced" the difference between being talkative and gregarious versus connecting with others at a deep and vulnerable level. It gave being unquiet a whole new meaning for me.

I can't say I've changed the world, but I do know that being unquiet has benefited me and other people in my life, and others not necessarily part of my life.

If I were not unquiet, I would probably not be me. I can't imagine, or even wonder, what or who I would otherwise be. There's no other possibility. Being unquiet is who I am.

**UN** ARE YOU READY TO BE
UNBORING?

# SHOWING UP AND MAKING A STATEMENT

> "I've lived such a great, fantastic life already, but there's still so much more."
>
> — Katy Perry

In the previous chapter, I encouraged you to lean in, speak up, and not allow any obstacle to get in the way of your speaking up about what you believe—now.

One reason I'm obsessed with working with on purpose individuals like you, people who are up to something bigger in this world than increasing their income, is I've witnessed so many incredibly intelligent and successful people get on stage or on camera and be absolutely boring and unable to deliver their ideas in ways that enrolled others into their causes.

I am taking a stand for you to be unboring. It's something I've spent my entire life studying and mastering. This chapter and the next will focus on the physical act of showing up and the X Factor beneath it.

First, we'll explore the practical side of speaking and leading.

## YOU SHOW UP WHERE YOU ARE (AND IT'S A CHOICE)

Practically speaking, people are always watching. Will you be there when they are watching?

Remember, while words are powerful, your actions (who you're being) are far more powerful and influential.

It's all too common in speaking and leadership for the speaker/leader of the moment to appear at the time of his delivery, when the spotlight is on him. And then, he is gone.

Some make an effort to appear at other times; however, their appearances are obviously cursory and almost forced. You can tell they are just out and about *shaking hands and kissing babies*.

I built the performing arts program at the high school where I taught for nearly a decade by being present. In fact, I would go so far as to say my teaching partner, Kathy, and I had to become nearly omni-present. We were both committed to the students and available to them. The result was a program that grew rapidly and raised up student leaders who influenced and inspired change in others.

We showed those students what it looked like to be a leader.

We showed up as a standing ovation for them, first.

## BEFORE THE STANDING OVATION

In all the years I've worked with performers, presenters, speakers, and leaders, I've observed a lot of standing ovations. I've also observed a lot of times when standing ovations did not happen. Can you predetermine a standing ovation?

The common mistake is thinking the standing ovation happens at the end of your delivery. In the theater, I didn't have the luxury of waiting for standing ovations; instead, I had to create them. Here's what I learned.

# SHOWING UP AND MAKING A STATEMENT

The standing ovation is something that takes time to produce. Whether or not it will happen is determined the moment you "take the stage."

If you want to increase your chances of creating an audience-moving experience, show up as a standing ovation for your audience. It's that simple.

In practical terms, showing up as a standing ovation would mean having the energy of someone who is giving a standing ovation as you enter the stage. Yes, *you* show up as the person giving a standing ovation for the audience. Have your speaker introduction written so that it both edifies you and creates initial connection with the audience. Include both professional accolades and more personal/human points to create that connection. For example, you may make a mention of where you grew up, where you went to school, where you live now, with whom, pets, what you love to do when you're not working. All of these details make you more accessible and real to your audience.

As you wait to get on stage, listen to the introduction and imagine that each member of the audience researched you and wrote it about you. Imagine that each audience member is the one who's actually introducing you.

As you enter the stage, have the energy of celebratory gratitude. You take a stand for the members of your audience and show up as if you were acknowledging them for the way they are acknowledging you in their applause and your introduction.

Never introduce yourself, and never leave the introduction to chance. Write it and give it to the planner or person who's introducing you and ask him or her to read it.

Never let the first words you say from the stage be, "Thank you. It's so great to be here." Instead, where appropriate, shift the focus on them. Acknowledge the event itself; celebrate the planners and the audience for their energy. If you did it correctly, you'd have arrived early and met some members of the audience—acknowledge that.

In most cases, I advise that you just start with your talk as planned. You've already been set up, so imagine how tedious it gets for audience members who have already sat through several speakers, or several days of speakers and presentations, where everyone starts the same way. Just start—they are waiting for you to deliver your vision.

The best thing you can do when you have a speaking engagement of any kind is to arrive early and be seen. A lesson I learned traveling the world and teaching young people is that the thing people want the most from you is your time and attention. Nothing matters more than you genuinely seeing and hearing your audience. Arriving early and, of course, staying after you present is the easiest way not only to connect with your audience, but to attract more opportunities. People in your audience will want to bring you in to speak and lead their groups. Showing up early and staying late will allow you to discover those opportunities and build relationships that will bear fruit in time.

Showing up early and staying late, believe it or not, is also a great bargaining chip when you are negotiating speaking engagements. When you connect personally with the event planners or committee, if you say you will arrive early to get to know their audience, stay late to sign books or answer questions, and appear at a special dinner or lunch, you set yourself apart from the vast majority of speakers who are only interested in flying in and out.

The performance world (speaking, leading, and performing) is largely led by ego. Ego is the killer of collaboration and community. It alienates audiences, and it feeds the ego-driven. Speakers and leaders who thrive on ego are the ones who believe they are the main attraction and make it known. They believe what they have to offer is valuable (more on value in Chapter 16) and that their time is equally valuable, so they make their appearance as per the contract and then are whisked away by their personal assistant, get on calls, or are visibly unpresent after they deliver. I'm sure you've all experienced this in some form.

## THREE KINDS OF SPEAKERS AND LEADERS

I've observed there are three types of speakers (including performers, presenters, and leaders) and three schools of thought:

1. **Gurus:** Gurus leverage their celebrity status (real, implied, or self-perceived) and exclusivity. These speakers believe they have a lot of value to deliver to audiences. They can be some of the more difficult personalities to deal with, and they are often the most expensive and/or demanding. They may arrive with an entourage, and they are generally not present outside the negotiated deliverables of their appearance contract.

2. **Mercenaries:** Mercenaries believe they are eternal servants. "It's all about the audience." Some mercenaries are actually gurus in disguise who have figured out that it's good marketing to say it's all about the audience and that they are there to serve, over-deliver, and be the vessel for others' success. Some mercenaries are authentic (in which case they shy away from accolades and will not easily receive standing ovations), while others are just good marketers who think making it all about others will win them more favor.

3. **Ambassadors:** Ambassadors understand that speaking and leading is an ecosystem; there is a balance. Their presence and message is just as important as the audience and what they believe. Ambassadors show the audience what it looks like to step into the light, they shine the light on others, and they empower and invite others to share in it. At the same time, they receive with class and grace. Ambassadors have knowledge, wisdom, and great humility, and they lead by example.

By now you've probably guessed what kind of speaker or leader you should be: the ambassador. This is what will best allow you to show up fully and to connect with your audience.

## YOU ARE ALREADY SEEN AND HEARD

Whether you are conscious of it or not, people are always watching and assessing. From your social media presence to the impromptu interaction you may have with someone in the grocery store, when you decide to step into the spotlight and become the ambassador for an idea, you live a public life.

On my last day of Teachers College, I sat through a presentation entitled "Life as a Teacher." The one thing from that presentation that was burned into memory was the statement, "The moment you walk outside this hall, your life will never be the same. Now you are a teacher, and you will be watched and judged differently. You have to *be* a teacher in public. You have to dress and act a certain way. You give up your regular life when you leave this hall."

Every cell in my body was having a reaction. I think I even turned to my friend and said, "I didn't sign up for this.... Can I get a refund?"

I hated the idea of having to play a character the moment I left my home. It felt disingenuous.

Of course, unapologetic me determined that the best way forward was simply to be a man of integrity and to be *myself* everywhere. I went so far as to tell my students on the first day of classes that I would be deeply offended if they saw me out and about and they ignored me. Of course, I didn't want to discuss class outside of class necessarily, but neither did I want them to think I became someone different inside the classroom.

When I signed up to become a teacher, I made a decision to be a leader. Leaders lead, speakers speak, and they are consistent in their commitment to their causes.

As a leader in your space, what are you committed to?

_____

_____

_____

Who do you need to be in order to lead and inspire others?

_____

_____

_____

## YOU SHOW UP WHERE YOU ARE

It's a lesson I learned the hard way, a few times. Running away from myself when I went to high school, fleeing to the Arctic, and even organizing my female fan club in kindergarten, I showed up.

*Showing up* isn't only about the physical act; it includes your thoughts, beliefs, and feelings. In other words, you have the choice to show up for others and for yourself at any given moment.

In the role of speaker, leader, and ambassador, showing up fully and with integrity (where integrity is being in alignment with what you say you will do or be) is the key ingredient to creating standing ovation moments.

When you show up unapologetically, transformation is possible. Steve Jobs understood this, and as a result, his legacy continues to transform people and his industry. He was committed to being the ambassador of his brand and belief: *Think Different*.

Leaders who create impact also believe there is always more. There is no *arrival*. There is only more journey. Katy Perry probably has enough money to retire if she wants. But her commitment to what she believes and how she expresses that gives her the inspiration to move forward to ongoing discovery and development. And her fans and followers get to receive the blessings of her belief and her ongoing expansion.

Celebrate where you've been. Celebrate where you are. Celebrate where you're going.

How can you incorporate more celebration in the way you show up for yourself and others?

_____

_____

_____

What effect will this change have on you and others?

_____

_____

_____

What are you celebrating right now?

_____

_____

_____

_____

# SPOTLIGHT: UNAPOLOGETIC INFLUENCER

## UNBORING

**BY VANESSA SHAW**

*Vanessa Shaw is a business coach, personal development junkie, and inspirational speaker all rolled up into one! You can learn more about her at VanessaShaw.com.*

For me, being unboring means living a life that feels exciting and extraordinary. It's not about accepting status quo or mediocrity but rather constantly seeking to improve myself, the value I bring to the world, and the life experiences I choose to live.

The notion of being unboring hit me in my early forties. I was enjoying a level of success in my own business and coaching top attorneys in a major European law firm on how to take their businesses and lives to the next level. These conversations quickly evolved into them declaring they wanted more challenges and new experiences in their personal and professional lives. As I coached them to break through their own limits and achieve their next level of success, I had to take a cold hard look at my own life and goals and be brutally honest that not only was I playing small, but my life had become very predictable and boring.

I was happily married with two children, two cars, two pets, and a four-bedroom house. There was nothing inherently wrong with all of that, except I felt I was living the quintessential middle-class existence that I'd been taught to expect.

When I gave myself permission to explore what was missing for me, I realized my life didn't feel adventurous, I wasn't excited about the future, and I had become a very bland version of myself.

This realization started me on a journey of digging deeper into my own desires and discovering that what I really wanted to do was leave Switzerland, where I had been living for almost twenty-one years, and pursue my dream to move to the United States.

I then literally turned my life upside down. I had to close down my business, get my children out of schools they'd been in for years, sell my house, and prepare to leave my husband behind for the next two years as I set up our new life in the United States. My husband would join me two years later when he finished his career at the United Nations.

Within eleven months of making the decision to move to the States, I arrived in Scottsdale, Arizona, in the middle of a very hot summer! Over the next four years, I pursued my dream of growing my business and built a seven-figure brand serving hundreds of entrepreneurs across multiple states.

It's been my honor to help so many of my clients break through their own limiting beliefs about who they think they should be in the world so they can become the people they really want to be deep down inside. Once that shift occurs, they become unapologetic about who they are, what they want, and how they show up in the world. The positive results always follow!

Personally, striving to be unboring has enabled me to build a brand around the tagline "Be Bold. Play Bigger." My clients expect me to be a role model of unboring and to show up differently. This, in turn, gives them permission to shine more brightly and demand more for themselves and the people they serve. Ultimately, being unboring has been a win-win situation for me and everyone I have the privilege to serve. It's simply too dull and boring to live life any other way.

**UN** ARE YOU READY TO BE
UNFORGETTABLE?

# BECOMING UNFORGETTABLE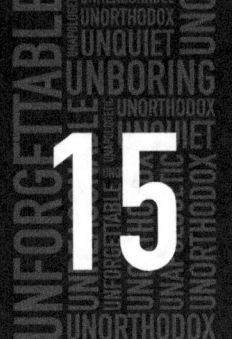

"Nothing strengthens authority so much as silence."

— Leonardo DaVinci

Creating an impact on the world requires the courage and vulnerability to show up. Being committed to what you believe, unapologetically, goes a long way in building your platform, developing your brand, and spreading your message and mission. When you choose to show up, as discussed in the last chapter, the outcome will always be growth and evolution of who you are, how you relate with the world, and how the world relates with you.

In an earlier chapter, I shared that part of my original brand was the word and idea of being "unforgettable." While "unforgettable" isn't the dominant driver today, it is still a major factor and one that people are always asking about. This chapter will look at how you can predictably engineer becoming unforgettable as a speaker and leader.

## THE AFFECTIVE DOMAIN OF LEARNING

It's no secret that emotion plays a major role in how people make decisions. It's the reason why storytelling has become such a hot topic for speakers and leaders alike.

To create an environment where you elicit specific emotions isn't always the easiest proposition. The ideal scenario is for you to create and deliver an experience that results in your audience saying (and feeling) "Wow."

Here's the reality when it comes to creating Wow experiences:

- Wow is not your content.
- Wow is a feeling.

The real secret lies in how to sustain the emotion created from your initial presentation or appearance.

Back in Chapter 10, I outlined the six levels of the cognitive domain of learning. We learned that remembering is the lowest function while creating is the highest function of the *thinking* part of the brain.

The emotional/feeling part of your brain is the affective domain. Receiving knowledge ranks at the lowest level of the affective domain.

Understanding the affective domain is your ticket to *Wow*. There are five levels of emotional engagement:

1. Receiving
2. Responding
3. Valuing
4. Organizing
5. Internalizing

In this section, we'll look at each one.

**Receiving:** The process of speaking may seem obvious: You, as the speaker or leader, have information to deliver, and your audience will receive it. It's important to consider, however, that true reception occurs when there is an agreement or willingness to receive. After all, unless the point of your talk or workshop is for your audience to be soothed by your voice, true receiving of your information is a critical factor in your out-of-the-gate success.

Establish a space where you create an agreement with your audience. Short of flat out asking for agreement and focus (which may be appropriate, depending on the audience), you can do this by having an opening so strong and compelling that people have no choice but to listen and be drawn in. It's absolutely critical that your opening—the moment you step on the stage—is a carefully crafted, energy-packed (not necessarily high energy, but focused energy) affair.

To have your audience "receive" is the lowest level of engagement when it comes to emotion, but if you aren't commanding attention, you are fighting an uphill battle to engage anyone at any deeper level.

**Responding:** Following suit, the next level of emotional engagement involves encouraging active participation through *response*. You need to supply the opportunity for response to occur. Besides the more obvious scenario of having people raise their hands or shout out something catchy, think about creating the opportunity for those in your audience to respond to what they have received by taking a poll, volunteering to be an example (can be quick and easy if you design it to be so), or participating in an audience challenge. Active participation requires a higher level of investment from the audience than simply receiving information (which can be going on while texting, tweeting, and taking selfies—sadly, I've seen all of this done during presentations and keynotes. I'm sure you've seen the same.)

When you give people in your audience the opportunity to respond to what they receive, you begin to require and encourage a deeper (and more impactful) level of personal investment—affective investment.

Now, a word on eliciting responses. If you're going to ask a question, make it a great question *and* wait for the genuine response/reaction.

Far too often, speakers (especially those trained in NLP) ask questions designed to enroll engagement, but they blow by the answers so fast that they are clearly not interested in the actual response. If you're asking for a response, wait for it; be present with your audience members and respond appropriately to how they respond!

**Valuing:** Eliciting audience participation is *not* about adding value. In order to get someone to value something, you need to have a way to measure acceptance of the idea you're sharing and (if you're really going for the golden wow) show evidence that there is a new commitment as a result of your information. "How?" you ask.

- Provide your audience with opportunities to address or solve problems that are real for them.

- Let bold statements land.

- Encourage silence while people process concepts.

- Frame your information, story, ideas, or teachings in such a way that the audience can relate.

- Remember, it's *not* only about you—it's about your perspective on what is valuable to them.

- In a workshop setting, or the kind of talk where it's appropriate for you to interact more, there is also huge value in giving people the opportunity to share their perspective in a safe, judgment-free space.

When you allow your audience members to self-establish value… they tell you the value! (Now that's valuable!) The key is always to frame things to be adaptable to your listeners to allow them access to personal affective relevance (what is important to them).

**Organizing:** You want your audience to accept different views/ideas, synthesize them, and develop a new understanding of ideas. In other words, to have an aha moment, your listeners need to organize the material in a way that allows them to see new potential for a change in behavior through the comparing, relating, and synthesizing of values. An easy way to get people to organize new ideas is to show comparisons:

- Old way of thinking vs. new way of thinking
- Before transformation and after transformation
- With your solution, and without your solution

It's in the demonstration of these kinds of comparisons that you create the opportunity for people to have their own aha moments which, in turn, lead to them organizing new ideas, behaviors, patterns, and pathways in their own minds.

In summary, if you provide the opportunity for aha (instead of you simply giving the answer), you will access the emotional response that most effectively brings about change.

**Internalizing:** Internalizing is the highest level, or, as I like to call it, "after aha." It's the resulting action that occurs once someone has received, responded (engaged in), placed value in, and self-realized (the aha). Because of the affective impact you've facilitated, your audience members will now prioritize time to meet the needs of this new realization, make space in their lives, and adjust and balance family, relationship, and professional needs to maintain and nurture the new behavior. When audiences internalize your ideas, they take action—they buy your product or service, they think differently, or they take the next steps you invite them to take.

Here's the key and where most speakers and entrepreneurs absolutely fall flat: The new value systems/ideas, now internalized, have the potential to consistently affect behavior if you nurture the relationship to do so.

Put simply, once you've converted a stranger into a follower or a client, or you've enrolled your audience, followers, or employees into a new idea, it is your responsibility to foster and encourage ongoing positive transformation. What you do *after* you leave the stage matters.

Even in a keynote situation, where pitching is not appropriate, I've seen speakers invite people to stay connected to continue the conversation. Smart.

Just as with the cognitive domain of learning, using even just a few concepts presented here can affect massive change. You will instantly increase the level of engagement and success potential for everyone who experiences your talks, workshops, or presentations of any kind.

Transform your audiences from "consumers of information" (in other words, a taker) to independent thinkers who value information as the doorway to personal success, freedom, happiness, [insert transformation or result you inspire here], and empower them to know they themselves are the keys for their own transformations. Be their ambassador.

## PREACHING TO THE CHOIR

As I write this chapter, I'm sailing the Pacific on a cruise ship headed for Alaska. Today, one of the events onboard is a passenger Pop Choir Performance. Quite fitting for what I'm about to discuss.

I know I'm preaching to the choir. That you decided to pick up a copy of this book and have read this far is proof that you are already a speaker and leader on a mission to create positive transformation for others around the world. I celebrate you for being on the journey and for your commitment to sharing your ideas and your heart unapologetically.

It's interesting to note my own development from musical director to composer, producer, director, creator, entrepreneur, teacher, yogi—every experience—has contributed to the whole and what I share with you here.

After working with my mentor, Fred, through my undergraduate degree, the most transformational experience that deepened my understanding of performance happened while I was working with a choir during my teaching practice and the meeting that followed with world-renowned choral composer and my personal hero, Eric Whitacre.

At the time, I was rehearsing a high school vocal ensemble that was preparing for a concert of Whitacre's music. Whitacre, himself, would visit the ensemble for a private rehearsal.

The piece we were preparing was *Lux Aurumque* (*Light of Gold*), a brilliantly haunting piece with rich harmonies. Having worked with choirs and in the musical theater world extensively, I was excited for the opportunity.

Then I noticed that although the ensemble members were singing the right notes mostly (hey, it was high school after all), a layer was missing. The performance lacked soul. Everything I had known to work prior to this experience to inspire *feeling* in music didn't seem to have the effect I had hoped.

One evening, as I studied the piece, I realized another whole performance layer was implied in the text and music—an emotional journey from beginning to end. If I could teach that, I would be able to support the ensemble in bringing the piece to life.

I began to draw out the piece graphically, as if I were drawing the contour of an expansive mountain range. I broke down each phrase of music into a contour, which existed in the larger arc that encompassed the piece from a beginning to middle to end perspective. Then I brought in the sketch to the next rehearsal, and I walked the ensemble through it, drawing it on the whiteboard, phrase by phrase.

It worked. Not only did the performance begin to breathe, but the students gained a deeper understanding, appreciation, and love for the piece. Understanding what I've come to call the "dynamic architecture" of the piece also increased their investment—they performed with more confidence, as if they knew a secret, and in their performance, they were unraveling the secret for the audience.

In that moment, I knew what I had discovered was my leading edge, and a big part of what Fred had taught me in a different way. I'd worked with and observed a lot of performers and directors, and it is usually this X Factor that I find missing.

Years later, I learned that Whitacre designs all of his compositions using what he calls "emotional architecture." Before he writes a single note of music, he sketches, ideates, brainstorms, and literally draws the piece and components of it graphically.

What is the practical application of this information for a speaker and leader?

Intention. Before you speak, before you lead others, ask yourself, "Where will I meet my audience" (or "Where are we right now, and where am I going to take them?") Then, reverse-engineer the experience you will facilitate for them.

## THE ATTITUDE OF CHAMPIONS

In the summer of 2014, I had an idea. I knew I was approaching the end of my teaching career and started branching out into other areas. That summer break, I took a trip to San Antonio, Texas, to watch the Drum Corps International Regional Championships.

When I was twenty, I had been a member of the Oakland Crusaders' Drum and Bugle Corps. It has since folded, and drum corps would have all but vanished in Canada if my good friend Michael Beauclerc had not decided to bring it back in a big way through scholastic drum lines. He continues to build the Canadian Drumline Association with great success, now with events across Canada.

If you don't know what drum corps is, think of a professional marching band putting together a Super Bowl worthy show that includes music, drill (choreography and formations on the field), dance, artistry, and a whole lot of imagination.

Even though I only marched one year, I enjoyed the activity and loved to watch performances when the opportunity would come up.

So, in 2014, as I was watching the twenty-two groups compete and sending images back to Michael for his social media channels and magazine, it occurred to me that some groups did not have the attitude of champions. When I observed them on the field, I could see they found the performance hard, not fun and joyful, and they simply didn't *look* or *act* like champions. (The difference was obvious when one of the top three groups would take the field.)

As soon as I returned from that trip, I reached out to my old friend Kelly Earp. I hadn't seen him in nineteen years, since we had marched together in drum corps. I simply told him I had an idea and wondered whether he was still involved in marching band or drum corps at any level.

As luck would have it, Kelly was a visual caption head for the Cary High School Marching Band in North Carolina, meaning he was one of the guys in charge of how the marching band looked on the field.

Over the next twenty-four hours, we went from not having spoken in nineteen years to me being offered the chance to come down to North Carolina for a couple of weeks to bring my experiment to life.

The idea was simple. I wanted to train members of the marching band to become champions, physically, mentally, and creatively, and I was going to do that using yoga as the platform.

As I taught very specific yoga sequences that would address the strength and stamina members would need to perform their show, I also introduced personal development concepts that would teach how to show up like a champion, how to add layers of dynamic architecture, how to be unmessable on the field even when things went wrong, how to express themselves creatively, and, ultimately, how to become a single living organism that worked together to wow the audience.

It worked. For only the second time in its history, the Cary High School Marching Band made it to the semi-finals at the Bands of America Championship.

What I discovered in this experiment (that I went on to repeat) is how much the power of belief is tied to being remembered and to becoming inspiring and influential.

Success is multi-faceted and largely rooted in mindset. Simply saying the right words will not sustain you for the long term. Being an unapologetic leader and speaker is a lifelong practice that includes physical, mental, and creative conditioning and growth. When it comes down to it, belief is the biggest determining factor in expanding your influence beyond that of others.

Are you willing to do and be what it takes to *become* a world-class speaker and leader?

In my experience, many say they want it, but they fall short when the reality of how much practice, rehearsal, commitment, and dedication is required sets in. The idea that you can get on stage and *crush it naturally* is like waiting to win the lottery. Acquiring leadership and speaking skills requires thousands of hours.

The most common comment I hear from those who don't come from a performance background when they observe their favorite actor, singer, or dancer is "They make it seem so natural and unrehearsed." Unfortunately, several "experts" in the speaking space encourage speakers not to over-practice. Yes, memorization word-for-word can suck the life and soul out of a talk. However, when you move from memorized to internalized, you achieve a whole new level of connection with your material and the freedom to be present for your audience.

In other words, if you want to look natural and create in the moment on stage, you need to practice so much that it becomes second nature and a part of who you are. Then go back and add that magical layer of dynamic architecture to your work, essentially, breathing life, space, and subtext (what you don't say) back into it.

As the quote by Leonardo DaVinci that opens this chapter insinuates, it's in the work that goes behind the words, the silent moments you take to discover who you are, and the moments where you are silent that your greatest power lies. When you show up as a champion, world leader, or speaker, people will take note. What are you waiting for?

Physically, what can you do to build the stamina and healthy practices needed to sustain you as a world-class speaker and leader?

_____

_____

_____

Mentally, what can you do to develop your success (and unmessable) mindset?

_____

_____

_____

Creatively, what can you do to stretch and grow your current worldview, experiences, and understanding of others?

_____

_____

_____

# SPOTLIGHT: UNAPOLOGETIC INFLUENCER

# UNFORGETTABLE
## BY JOIE CHENG, MSW

*Joie Cheng is a professional keynote speaker, best-selling author, and transformational book publishing coach. You can learn more about her at JoieCheng.com.*

To be unforgettable is to know you will be remembered because you have created a legacy that outlives you. To become unforgettable, you must be willing to allow yourself to be seen and heard by sharing your naked truth with the world.

I used to fear that when I died, I would be forgotten. Writing and publishing my book, *The Naked Truth: A Woman's Journey to Self-Love*, has given me peace in knowing that I can never be forgotten now because my life will live on through my book long after I am physically gone.

The best way to be unforgettable is to share your story because there has never been and never will be again someone like you. You have a unique story to share. I encourage you to share your story, maybe even write your transformational book so you know that when you die, you will not be forgotten—your legacy and impact will live on through your book.

Being unforgettable happens when you make an impact on people by doing something outside the norm. For example, I decided to be naked on my book cover because I bare my soul in my book and wanted the cover to reflect that. I've had a lot of people tell me I'm brave for being naked on my cover. I tell them it was scarier to be naked in my book by baring my soul. Although it wasn't necessarily the original intention, being naked on my book cover has made me unforgettable because it catches people's attention. It goes against the norm.

I used to be afraid of being myself fully because I was afraid of rejection. What I didn't realize then was that the people who liked me only liked the me I was allowing them to see, not the real me. When I wrote my book, I let the real me shine for all to see, and it has attracted so many people to my story that it has confirmed for me that the real me is unforgettable too.

How can you be unforgettable? Let me give you an example by sharing the story of someone in my life who became unforgettable to me. Ever since I had visited San Diego in high school, I'd had a dream of living there. I loved the nice weather and palm trees, especially since I had grown up in the Chicago suburbs where we only got warm weather three months out of the year—if we were lucky. In 2013, one of my acquaintances who lived in the San Diego area told me that I should come live with her and her husband since she knew I wanted to live in San Diego and they had an extra bedroom. I told her that first I needed a job. She said she knew lots of people, so she told me to tell her how much money I needed to make and what kind of job I wanted, and she would help me find a job. I told her I didn't really know anyone in San Diego, so I needed friends. She reminded me that she knew lots of people so she said to tell her what kinds of friends I wanted and she would help me find friends. Then I told her I didn't know what to say. "Just say yes," she replied. I felt like the universe was giving me my dream on a silver plate, and if I didn't say yes now, then the next time I asked the Universe for something, it probably wouldn't give it to me, so I said yes. When I asked my acquaintance why she was doing this for me, she said "Because someone did it for me when I moved to San Diego, so I'm paying it forward." Her generosity was so "out of the norm" that she became unforgettable to me, and I will always be grateful for her help.

Being unforgettable has benefited me because it has attracted my highest paying clients, doubled my income, increased my speaking opportunities, and gotten me podcast interviews. Today, my story has been heard in almost every country in the world, and it has allowed me to leave a legacy that will impact people forever. Being unforgettable by sharing my story has inspired others to share their stories, which, ultimately, has created more healing in the world.

I encourage you to become unforgettable by sharing your story. We only have a short time on this planet to make the biggest impact possible. Don't waste your time. Instead, leave an unforgettable legacy.

# UN ARE YOU READY TO BE UNORTHODOX?

# MEASURING YOUR VALUE 16

"I woke up and liked myself today. Your like is extra. My job is to like me first!"

— Lisa Nichols

In the last chapter, I offered some tools to allow you to craft your talks so they will stimulate the highest levels of the feeling part of the brain: the affective domain. Understanding how to take your audience from simply receiving information to internalizing it is a skill (and an art) that will set you apart from other speakers and leaders.

Speaking to that, how will you know when you are becoming more influential, more followed, more understood than anyone else in your industry? What is the measure by which you determine your success?

## COMPARANOIA STRIKES AGAIN (AND AGAIN)

The need to be validated often stirs up feelings of comparanoia. Measuring success or impact may cause you to have a variety of feelings that do not serve you, such as:

- I'm not as good as...
- I'm not good enough...

- When I achieve X, I'll be successful...(and then what?)
- I need to do more...
- I need to get better at...
- I haven't put in my time at...

For some, these thoughts and feeling are enough to cause them to abandon their causes. Especially if they are not working in their zones of genius, it will be a long, bumpy road to feeling like they've *arrived* (if they ever do).

When in doubt, look back at your *Everyday Extraordinary Storytelling Book* and celebrate! Remember, all the breadcrumbs are there. The hints and clues that demonstrate who you are and why you are who you are will bring you back into alignment. I speak from experience.

When I first arrived in the United States of America, I decided to take on the role of complete student. I didn't want to pretend to know anything. Instead, I chose to absorb and learn from other successes.

I watched webinars, attended seminars, signed up for courses, attended events, and as you can imagine, spent a lot of money along the way.

Perhaps it was the timing of it, or maybe I had never had the time to notice before that there were a lot of experts online who all promised the exact, step-by-step formula to success.

So I followed.

## ADDING VALUE

The one thing I kept seeing over and over again was the message that in order to make it, if you really want to stand out and build a business of any kind, you have to put out content, add value, and, in fact, over-deliver on value.

# MEASURING YOUR VALUE

I found this concept rather unusual. No one had ever asked me to add value. I started to wonder if this was an American thing. As I considered the value I brought to the world, I looked back on my life. Here's what I discovered:

- I'm highly educated (two degrees, one diploma, advanced studies at five well-known institutions)—for whatever it's worth
- My resume is filled with achievements across multiple industries, including awards, recognition, and in-depth firsthand experiences—again, for whatever it's worth
- I'm a miracle, no matter which way you slice it—religion or science—I'm a miracle and so are you

That, in itself, seemed pretty valuable to me, but I know it's not what the gurus meant. I decided to look up the meaning of "value" because I couldn't exactly figure out how to determine what was deemed valuable.

When I looked up the definition of value, a few things really stood out for me, including *merit*, *worth*, and *importance*. So I asked myself:

- What is the merit of what I bring to the table?
- Am I worth your time, investment, endorsement?
- How important am I or the content I produce?

It's clear that these questions all come from a perspective of lack and scarcity. Looking at my own life through the lens of value's definition, I realized I had been ranked, judged, chosen last, dumped, and even disowned—none of those ever feel good. Why would anyone want to measure his or her value? When do you arrive at being valuable enough? And who decides?

I decided this idea that success is determined by your *value* was unacceptable and went on to do further research on what real value was.

As a kid, I was quite the researcher. I had even won a couple of science fairs. The boy scientist in me had now woken and I got to work.

Of course, one of the easiest ways today to conduct research is to use the internet. I made a single post on my Instagram and Facebook accounts that requested "Name someone prominent who delivers value."

The answers started pouring in: Gary Vaynerchuk, Russell Brunson, Tony Robbins, Brené Brown. These people certainly seemed like they delivered value. There were other answers like Bruce Springsteen, which seemed to be an interesting choice. One woman said "my husband," also an interesting choice. And another woman said Mahatma Gandhi. When I asked her why she felt he delivered value to her, she replied, "Because he showed me you can be small and brown like me and still change the world!"

In other words, no one had a clear measure for what value really is. Why then would you want to use value as a measurement at all? It's a moving target and very subjective.

As I looked closely at the people who were nominated, I started to see a pattern that ties everything together.

## DELIVERING VISION

Is it possible that vision has currency in the modern marketplace? That is the question I next set out to find the answer to.

Consider some of the modern visionaries of the day. Indicate if you believe these people deliver vision, value, or both:

|  | VISION | VALUE | BOTH |
|---|---|---|---|
| Elon Musk | _____ | _____ | _____ |
| Mother Teresa | _____ | _____ | _____ |

# MEASURING YOUR VALUE

Richard Branson    _____    _____    _____
Walt Disney        _____    _____    _____
Oprah Winfrey      _____    _____    _____
Dalai Lama         _____    _____    _____
Brené Brown        _____    _____    _____

Choose some of your own heroes, influencers, and those you hold in high regard and apply the same measure:

|  | VISION | VALUE | BOTH |
|---|---|---|---|
| _____ | _____ | _____ | _____ |
| _____ | _____ | _____ | _____ |
| _____ | _____ | _____ | _____ |
| _____ | _____ | _____ | _____ |
| _____ | _____ | _____ | _____ |
| _____ | _____ | _____ | _____ |
| _____ | _____ | _____ | _____ |
| _____ | _____ | _____ | _____ |

What can you conclude based on your results?

_____
_____
_____

I've conducted this experiment with audiences and people around the world. The results always lean toward showing that *people who have strong vision also deliver value*.

## VISION IS VALUABLE

I have a pretty firm belief that content is *not* actually king—you are. I can get nearly all the content I could ever want for free from Google. Google is king and queen when it comes to content with no end in sight to its global reign.

I don't know about you, but I prefer not to go head to head with Google because I know I will never be able to measure up, at least not for the long term.

What makes *you* stand out and be more *valuable* than the next expert in your space? Vision.

You are the key. People are waiting for you to reveal your vision.

The added beauty about vision is that it is exempt from measurement. Vision is total and singular all at the same time. One vision isn't better than the other. The currency of vision is binary.

Andrew Lloyd Webber, the famous composer of record-breaking musical plays, said, "What strikes me is that there's a very fine line between success and failure. Just one ingredient can make the difference."

The difference is vision. Having a vision will better position you for success than any other element.

Do you have a vision? Does your vision guide everything you do?

You may be starting to see how *vision*, *who* you are, and your *why* are all closely tied together.

When it comes to dealing with comparanoia, vision and a deep understanding of who you are and why you are who you are will all serve you in taking your stand with confidence, class, and longevity.

You, just like the visionaries you follow and celebrate, have the potential to create impact on others when you declare and share your vision, and when your vision is in alignment with who you are and what you believe, you become unstoppable.

A friend of mine, Doctor Vidya Reddy, is a woman on a mission with a clear vision. Here is what she has to say about vision:

> I believe every human being is worthwhile. It has been my plight in this life to give a voice to the voiceless. I have helped educate countless little girls in India to go from abject poverty to boundless possibilities!
>
> I'm a naturopathic doctor. When I was twenty-four, I traveled to India, where I was guided and initiated by master gurus, who took a simple Canadian girl and showed her the true meaning of giving. They cracked my heart wide open.
>
> Because I have seen countless people who have lost their inner voice, lost their joy, and lost their happiness, I created a program, *How to Become Naturally Happy* to teach people how to do exactly that. This program is all about sharing the profound knowledge of joyous, healthy, and peaceful living! (Naturally-Happy.com)
>
> My goal is to awaken the human consciousness and to empower humankind again, by making you aware of the potential that lies within each and every human being! Anytime we get close to the heart of a common man, we get close to the soul of our vision.

Do you have a clear vision? Is your vision in alignment with who you are?

Think back to your *Everyday Extraordinary Storytelling Book*. Think back to the question, "So what? What do I want them to do about it?" as you applied it to each of your stories/incidents. What is your "Because I believe X, I want you to Y" statement? Consider all these things and brainstorm your vision—the one that will guide everything you say and do.

On the lines below, brainstorm your vision. Similar to your brand and what you believe, express the bigger picture of the work you are up to.

_____

_____

_____

_____

_____

_____

What's it going to take for you to stop waiting and stop measuring your value? Lisa Nichols says it best in the quote that opens this chapter: Your job is to like you first. Are you willing to choose you first? Or will you carry on waiting for likes and acknowledgments on social media? Are you going to wait for others to validate your vision, your miracle, your being?

I invite you to stop delivering value since it's quite clear that when you play the value and validation game, you will never arrive. There is no end in sight.

Stop delivering value. Start delivering vision.

Be unorthodox. Choose to deliver vision. Celebrate the successes of the visionaries who have paved the way for you. Stake your claim and move forward confidently because those who deliver vision, those unashamed and steadfast in the way they choose to show up for others, are the ones who lead the world.

# MEASURING YOUR VALUE

What are you celebrating right now?

_____

_____

_____

_____

_____

_____

# SPOTLIGHT: UNAPOLOGETIC INFLUENCER

## UNORTHODOX
**BY SARAH-NADA ARFA**

*Sarah-Nada Arfa is a speaker, coach, bodyworker, Forrest yoga teacher, and attorney. You can find out more about her at SarahNadaArfa.com.*

To me, being unorthodox means a few things:

1. Choosing to be on and evolve off beaten tracks laid out before me by my beliefs, culture, society, religion, environment, and background.
2. Being and offering an alternative, a solution and service.
3. Being open to hearing and learning different opinions, thoughts, and methods.

Being unapologetically unorthodox means sharing my unorthodoxy loudly and proudly. It means being who I am, and listening to another with an open mind and heart so we can take our relationship, be it professional or personal, off the beaten track and onto a creative and innovative avenue.

To be unorthodox takes courage. It took me a lot of courage and two near-death experiences to fully embrace my unorthodoxy. I fully adopted unorthodoxy because I did not have any choice in the matter. I felt it was either choosing/accepting being myself and, therefore, unorthodox or checking out from this planet. I chose to embrace my unorthodoxy because it sounded less radical and painful than dying, and now that I've done it, I must say that I fully recommend it.

Don't get me wrong; it was not easy to embrace being different, unconventional, unusual, abnormal, and in full integrity with myself or what I thought was myself. I am a woman of North African and Muslim origins. I grew up in Algeria and immigrated with my family to France following the Algerian Civil War (1991-2002).

As a child and then as a young adult, I quickly learned that standing out and being unorthodox was not the way to survive. In the streets of Algiers, standing out would have meant being catcalled or even harassed—and that's a best-case scenario. It was even believed that no one should even hear the voice of a woman because it was a betrayal of her modesty and good education. In the midst of the civil war, my survival depended on blending in.

As an immigrant, I did all I could to assimilate, or "integrate," as the French love to call it. This process again made being myself and, therefore, different, a real hurdle. I needed to jump over every step of the way, in school, during ID checks in the street by national police forces, when looking for my first flat or job, or when falling in love.

So I blended in as much as I could, repressing my originality and inherited unorthodoxy. Doing so allowed me to survive and even do well, but through that process, I had forgotten to live. I gagged on every spurt of unorthodoxy I could feel. I settled for working in a private practice and being everything everyone expected from a corporate finance lawyer.

Still, those spurts of unorthodoxy were sometimes too hard to resist, and when they erupted, they brought with them immense joy and abundance. For example:

- I decided, against all odds, to abandon the idea of engineering school at eighteen and leave France for London, where I decided to study law. There I lived the best years of my life so far in a city.

- After my stroke at age twenty-four, I went on a Southeast Asia tour with friends, against medical advice, where I not only forged lifelong bonds, but also fell in love with the region.

- When I joined a yoga retreat, which turned out to be bodyworkers training, in the north of England, it gave me a totally new understanding of healthcare, in general, and of my own body. I saw how it offered help to so many patients abandoned by traditional medicine.

- I could not help but sit on a Pilates ball in my office.

I was able to keep smiling and stay positive even in the darkest hours of hard work, heartaches, long hours, lack of sleep, betrayals, and stress from life, clients, and career.

So when I was faced with death the second time in January 2017, on my ICU bed in Austin, Texas, alone, I had no choice but to reflect on my past, on my regrets, on what I wanted to continue doing more of, and what I wanted to change. I realized all these situations had a common denominator: I was suffering from having dissociated from my true essence, from being my unapologetically unorthodox self. From that moment on, I decided to live unapologetically and be unorthodox. How did that materialize? I reclaimed what made my spirit sparkle: having fun; letting my wild imagination run free through making art and writing a children's book; practicing and teaching yoga; sharing my experiences by assisting others to reconnect with their breath, minds, bodies, and souls; embracing my coaching skills while staying an active member of the local and business community; and being of service to others. I realized I did not have to choose between all those parts of myself, even if those parts were at odds with what people expected from a female, Arab, Muslim lawyer!

Being unorthodox should not be just reserved for woo-woo artsy people. Being unorthodox is for everyone, and could even be a business/corporate advantage!

As a corporate finance lawyer, I have often found the best solutions for my clients' matters, questions, and issues come from my ability to stay within the confines of the law and still present them with unorthodox answers or solutions that fully meet their business needs. Doing so has also given me a strong competitive edge over anyone else who has a similar product or service to offer.

And I have seen the same show up in everything I do: as a yoga and bodyworker, as a coach, as a public speaker. People will come to me because of who I am and because I am not shy about it. If they don't like it, then they do not contact me, and that frees my time and energy to help and serve those who are a better fit and need me the most.

If you want to aim for the stars, being unorthodox shows your uniqueness to the world, and the world will then shower you with abundance and ease! Don't settle for what you or other people expect from you.

You can follow the path you think you should follow or go straight to where you want to be by getting off the beaten track! Ninety-nine percent of the time, I have found that the journey is less painful and quicker if you get off the beaten track, and it's way more fun! And isn't that what life is about? Making it worth our while by enjoying the ride?

**UN** ARE YOU READY TO BE
UNREASONABLE?

# LEADING WITH VISION

## 17

> "We cannot teach people anything; we can only help them discover it themselves."
>
> — Galileo Galilei

If you ask me, the most important thing you should measure is the quality of your daily celebrations—your own vision and intrinsic value (the miracle of you). Having a vision gives you a baseline, a true north, and it sends a clear message to others that you are living on purpose.

When you decide to stop being attached to value and being validated, and you choose vision as your guide, others will take note and you will find yourself in the position of leader and influencer.

My entire life experience as a leader is perfectly summed up in Galileo's words. Especially when I took on a leadership role as a high school music teacher, I quickly realized that my formative training in becoming a teacher was not very practical.

This chapter will explore true leadership—the kind of leadership that inspires and raises up other leaders.

I want you to know that nothing I share here is a prescription, nor is it meant to be interpreted as a formula. As I've expressed previously, I'm a firm believer, when it comes to speaking and leading, that there is no clear path. There are ideas and ideologies, skills, tactics, and methods that may work for you; however, it's up to you to pick and choose what works for you. Discover your leadership and style. Facilitating that discovery—unleashing someone's unique style—is what I love to do with clients.

As you read this chapter, consider who you want to be as a speaker and leader. What do you want others to say when you've left the room?

## BEING UNREASONABLE

I want you to be unreasonable, but not in the traditional sense; rather, what areas are you willing to explore and who are you willing to be in order to lead others to their own greatness? It's been my experience that having an unreasonable approach can be the most effective way to establish your leadership (and the depth of your message).

The very first day I taught high school music, I announced that the band would be performing a concert in two weeks. In fact, in later years, my teaching partner Kathy and I took this idea a step further by having students play music, sing live, and perform choreographed dance by the end of the first week of school!

I'm sure the rest of the teaching staff (and student body for that matter) thought we were crazy. Our students, however, loved it. They were inspired by our radical leadership and intensity. Every year, the performance went off without a hitch, and it positioned the performing arts department as a leading program—one to be a part of.

Kathy and I also had moments when we would sing with our students and be involved in large production numbers, not to showcase our own talents, but to demonstrate community, collaboration, and equity. Singing and dancing in front of your peers as a teenager is no small feat. By joining our students as cameo performers, we showed them that we believed in them, and if it was going to go terribly, we would also bear the criticism.

Luckily, we always wowed our audiences. Here's the interesting part. I can honestly say that the wow factor wasn't always because the performances were impeccable. I believe the wow factor and the respect that followed was a byproduct of who we were being—audacious, bold, and unapologetic. As teachers, we inspired our students by being unstoppable. Observing our bold attitude inspired our students, in turn, to follow *and* be unashamed—to be confident in who they were.

When I became a teacher, I knew one thing for sure: I wanted my program to be experiential because the experiences I'd had in high school were what had literally saved my life. My vision for my students was to facilitate immersive experiences—and so I did.

After successful first month performances, I decided to announce an international trip. Again, I'm 100 percent sure the other teaching staff thought I was absolutely out of my mind. Planning a trip to the local amusement park was a feat few teachers wanted to try to pull off, let alone planning international travel. I, however, was fearless (or naive) and carried on with the announcement of a Cuba arts experience for spring break.

Sixteen students followed my lead and traveled to Cuba that year. It was an immersive experience that positively impacted their lives.

The following years brought many more experiences: field trips to watch plays and musicals, workshops at the opera, backstage tours, dance workshops with the cast of *Jersey Boys*, an annual trip to Disney World, and an exchange trip with a school in Alberta, Canada (a town the size of our student body).

People wondered how I pulled all this off. I was unreasonable. To be clear, I didn't work at an affluent school, there was no booster program or heavy parent involvement, and there was no real budget ($0).

I used my experience as a composer as the blueprint for leading my students and the program to grow. In composition, you begin with nothing...a blank page. Then an idea begins to flourish, and slowly, something is created out of nothing. If I wanted to purchase a new instrument or equipment, I had to create it. If I wanted to bring in my friends from the professional world to do audition workshops, dance, stage combat, and drumming workshops, I had to create the opportunity—something from nothing.

It all started with vision, never enough time, and an unstoppable (often unreasonable attitude).

Being unreasonable allowed us to grow the program multiple times over, more than tripling it within a few years. The vision we had for the program was simple, "It's all about the kids." That simple phrase guided us and led us to success. It also inspired others (students *and* teachers) to follow.

You may be wondering how exactly you get a teenager to follow you. The answer turned out to be rather simple. We allowed only one option: saying "Yes."

We would actually joke with our students that we'd create T-shirts that said, "The answer is Yes." Upon further consideration, we realized this could lead to a bit of a public relations disaster (Think about it; do you really want to teach impressionable minds that the answer is always yes?), so we modified our mantra to, "The answer is Yes (and sometimes, rarely, no)."

It served us well. Not only did we establish our leadership platform, but we raised up leaders by our example. When you are absolutely obsessed with a vision, people take note (even teenagers). Vision is inspiring, and it spills over to others. People want to be a part of something bigger. We created that something and empowered others to step into the role of leaders inside the bigger vision.

## TEACHING HAS VERY LITTLE TO DO WITH TEACHING

Based on its name, you'd think that Teachers College is designed to teach you how to teach. Don't get me wrong—looking back there were certainly elements of practical teaching included in the program; however, most of what we did was more theoretical and based on learning behavior and human development. Useful stuff, though as a first year teacher, the more pressing things on my mind were, "How do I survive the first year?", "What exactly do I teach them?", and "How do I decipher the curriculum and board expectations?"

Fairly quickly, I came to learn that being a good teacher would actually require me to understand learning. I had to become an expert in learning so I could teach others how to learn for themselves.

It's such an important point to understand in order to be effective as a teacher, leader, or speaker.

You have a lot of knowledge. The tendency is to share it, to help people get the answers they need. Teaching others translates to delivering value, or so you would think. The problem is that when you hand someone the answer to something, for the most part, that person will not internalize it. It will be information that may or may not be remembered or even used for the longer term.

Notice how when you are the passenger in a vehicle, and later you become the driver, it's much harder to remember the directions. As a passenger, you are not having the experience of navigating for yourself.

Both teaching and learning work the same way.

## LEADERS LEAD. SPEAKERS SPEAK.

Give your students, followers, and clients the opportunity to have their own learning experiences. You facilitate the experiences and their subsequent learning and transformation.

Instead of simply delivering information, tell stories that have the lessons embedded within. Allow your audience members to analyze and organize for themselves. Give space for your followers to innovate and personalize.

As a leader, your role isn't to tell everyone what to do and how to do it. You are charged with leading others, supporting, cheering on, asking questions that inspire personal growth and development, building a platform of inclusion, and demonstrating integrity (doing what you say) and following through.

In my research of renowned leaders and visionaries, I have discovered a number of common character traits and habits. Here are the five most prominent:

1. **The focus to stay in your own lane:** Vision—having one and sticking to it. Not falling victim to comparanoia and jumping on the bandwagon for the next big thing. While there are countless highly successful people out there who constantly reinvent themselves and can be found endorsing the latest craze as it arises, the most successful people are always the ones who have clarity in what they are up to in this world, and they are experts at saying no to anything that would distract them.

2. **The willingness to do whatever it takes:** How far are you willing to go to bring your vision to life? Are you willing to send a Tesla into outer space to demonstrate your commitment to innovative technologies as Elon Musk did in early 2018? Are you willing to get back up after losing everything, like Walt Disney did after walking away from his creation Oswald the Lucky Rabbit, which came before Mickey Mouse, or as I decided to move forward in the aftermath of losing everything after lightning struck my home and burnt it to the ground? Are you willing to do whatever it takes to realize your vision?

3. **The ability to ask for and receive support:** Leaders don't do everything; in fact, it's a proven fact that the more suc-

cess one builds, the less tactical one becomes. How much are you doing yourself right now that you could probably outsource? How often do you think or feel you have to do it yourself to get it done right? How easy is it for you to ask for support?

4. **The confidence to take the first leap (to show others what it looks like):** Leaders lead. Speakers speak. For years, I thrived as the man behind the curtain, making only compulsory appearances. As I stepped more into my own power, I started to realize I was doing myself a disservice. I was also doing *you* a disservice. If I did not become the example, the number one ambassador for being unapologetic, how could I ever expect anyone else to do so? Today, I know it is my responsibility to take the first steps, to show you what it looks like, then to inspire you to follow as I support you in expressing and leading in your own unique way.

5. **An unapologetic commitment to who you are being for others:** Dolly Parton is the epitome of unapologetic. She carries no airs about the way she looks, how she talks, or what she does. She shows up fully as herself and has built a wildly successful career doing so. Donald Trump is equally unapologetic, and whether you like it or not (this is not meant to be a political statement), his way of being and commitment to that way are, in my opinion, the determining factors that allowed him to build traction and create a following to get himself elected President of the United States.

## WHO ARE YOU WILLING TO BE?

Who are you willing to be when it comes to your vision? Are you willing to be one of the *crazy ones* Steve Jobs talked about in the famous Think Different campaign? Are you willing to do what it takes to achieve your vision even when it gets uncomfortable? Are you willing to become the person who will stand out even when others say things that would make you want to hide behind the curtain?

Galileo Galilei was persecuted for his vision and for what he believed. He was silenced, in fact. He came to understand that sometimes having a big vision, regardless how positive it might be, can cause backlash. He would also come to understand, as he's quoted as saying, that the best way to present ideas is to lead others to their own discoveries. Perhaps, instead of declaring his discoveries, he could have approached others with information and inquiry that would have allowed them slowly to change their own minds... to consider for themselves what they believed was true about the universe. (Was the earth really at the center of it all?)

Leading with vision isn't about declaring what you believe and waiting for followers. Leading with vision is about believing so strongly in something that you are willing to present it in such a way that your audience members ultimately choose to believe it, not because you've told them to, but because you've given them the choice to do so.

Leading with vision is a powerful tool. Understanding that leading with vision actually means you are leading with who you are being, as opposed to a personal agenda, is even more powerful.

Think about what you believe. Think about your vision and mission. Why should others believe the same or jump on board? Why would someone else benefit from believing what you believe, knowing what you know, and being who you see them to be?

_____

_____

_____

What are you celebrating right now?

_____

_____

# SPOTLIGHT: UNAPOLOGETIC INFLUENCER

## UNREASONABLE

**BY BRIAN K. WRIGHT**

*Brian K. Wright is the host of Success Profiles Radio and the publisher of Success Profiles Magazine. You can learn more about him at BrianKWright.com.*

To be unreasonable is to refuse to accept mediocrity, to demand the best of yourself and others, and to have audacious goals and strategies that most would never consider for themselves. To be unreasonable is to be willing to make supreme sacrifices along the way. Unreasonable people don't *accept* what is; they *create* what could be.

Many people ask me what it takes to be successful. I could give a number of answers, but I heard one recently that made me stop and think, and that's what I want to address here.

I was at a fundraising event recently where Kevin Harrington from *Shark Tank* was speaking. At the end of the night, everyone who spoke stood on stage and talked about his or her big takeaway. One of them said, "All successful people are willing to do *bizarre* and *unreasonable* things." Out of everything that was shared that night, that's the one thing that stuck out for me.

Anyone who's ever achieved anything remarkable in life has been willing to do something many people would consider to be bizarre and unreasonable. I believe successful people need to be willing to be bizarre and unreasonable in three different areas in order to achieve their greatest aspirations. Those areas are: goals, sacrifices, and strategies.

## GOALS

The invention of the airplane certainly fits into the goals category. At the time, people were transporting themselves on the ground. Many of the Wright brothers' detractors were saying that if man were meant to fly, he would have wings, and that flying was literally for the birds. But the Wright brothers didn't listen; instead, they tried and tried and failed and tried and tried and failed and finally succeeded.

Similarly, when Henry Ford invented the Model T and made cars available to the masses, many people thought it was a very bizarre and unreasonable thing to do. People were traveling in horse-drawn carriages at the time. In fact, Henry Ford once said, "If I had asked people what they wanted, they would have said faster horses."

So you have to think a lot bigger. Having bizarre and unreasonable goals is certainly very important in achieving success.

## SACRIFICES

In addition, sometimes the sacrifices you have to make are going to be a little bizarre and unreasonable. For example, Elon Musk poured his own money into both Tesla and Space X. In fact, sometimes he poured so much of his own money into these companies that he didn't have money to pay his rent. As a result, he would sleep on people's couches. Wouldn't you think being homeless is a bizarre and unreasonable thing to do to honor your dream? I absolutely think so. I'm always amazed by some of the bizarre and unreasonable sacrifices successful people commit to in order to make their dreams come true.

## STRATEGIES

Not only do our goals and sacrifices have to be bizarre and unreasonable, but sometimes our strategies have to be so as well; that's how you become really, really memorable. So let me share a couple of brief examples.

Recently, I interviewed Tana Goertz from *The Apprentice*. She was the season three runner up. We talked about what it was like to meet Trump and work with him, and I asked her what impressed her about him. In preparation for the interview, I watched her *Apprentice* audition reel; she had actually auditioned for season two but hadn't made it. But her audition reel was amazing. At the time of her audition, she was very actively working in the Mary Kay organization, so part of her audition reel showed her going to car dealerships to sell Mary Kay products to the car salesmen before Mother's Day. It was a savage move, and she got kicked out of some of those dealerships for solicitation.

What I loved was that Tana was talking to guys about buying Mary Kay products for their girlfriends and mothers. She didn't take no for an answer. She was very professional. She wasn't a nuisance about it. If you want to see this video, go to YouTube and search "Tana Goertz *Apprentice* audition." It's really pretty amazing, yet bizarre and unreasonable. Who thinks of selling Mary Kay by going to car dealerships? It was actually a really, really great idea, especially since Tana had a thick enough skin to put up with rejection.

Another strategy I think is absolutely brilliant and savage involves the Girl Scouts. I will never forget one year during Girl Scout cookie season in February, I saw Girl Scouts selling cookies at a table in front of a bank on a Friday afternoon. That is bizarre, unreasonable, and totally brilliant because everyone coming out of the bank has money!

Ask yourself this: What unreasonable things can you do in terms of your goals, the sacrifices you're willing to make, and the strategies you're willing to implement?

You have to pay a price for whatever you do. If you decide you are willing to do only certain things but not others, you may not want your dream very badly. You can't put limitations on what you're willing to sacrifice in order to make your dreams come true. You have to have a very, very strong *why* in order to succeed on a massive scale.

So again: What bizarre and unreasonable goals, sacrifices, and strategies are you willing to implement to make your dreams come true?

If you're looking for validation and approval from the masses, you're only going to accomplish what the masses are accomplishing. So don't be afraid. Your greatness is only one decision away.

**UN** ARE YOU READY TO BE
UNSTOPPABLE?

# BEING UNSTOPPABLE 18

"If you don't like the road you're walking, start paving another one."

— Dolly Parton

For more than twenty-five years, I've observed and studied performers, leaders, and speakers who have created deep impacts on audiences around the world. How do they do it?

The X Factor of great leaders is their ability to be committed to who they are. Being Unapologetic isn't just a book title. It's a path to success that has long been proven by the world's most influential personalities.

From Jesus to Gandhi, Disney to Musk, and Ellen and Oprah to Mandela and Mother Teresa, and beyond, visionaries have led the way with their commitment to who they are *and* who they are being for others.

Being unapologetic isn't for the faint of heart. There will be challenges every step of the way. People will give unsolicited advice to play small, fall in line, go slow, and not push the boundaries.

*But those who are meant for big things have a calling.*

You know who you are. You've always known it.

The only difference between you and [insert your favorite leader or visionary here] is that he or she, as Dolly Parton suggests, paved another way—multiple times, in most cases.

That person chose to be unstoppable.

That person chose to be unapologetic about his or her vision because that vision was so big that it pulled him or her forward.

Over a lifetime of experiences and interactions, it's been my observation that the reason people fail isn't because they didn't get a break, aren't talented enough, or aren't in the right place at the right time. It's that they simply aren't unapologetic enough. Most people are *messable*. Instead of paving a new way, they scrap the entire journey.

Identify times in your life when you've scrapped an idea for whatever reason:

_____

_____

_____

_____

If you were to pave a new road for an idea, vision, or mission you abandoned earlier in your life, what would that new road look like?

_____

_____

_____

_____

## THE X FACTOR IS A CHOICE

Among the thousands of people I've studied, observed, and worked with, it has become extremely clear that the X Factor is rarely based in luck or genetics. It's a choice.

The choice is to be you, unapologetically, and to be unstoppable and unwavering in that choice. The more you choose *you*, the more you allow your miracle to shine through.

I knew in kindergarten that I was up to something bigger. That is not to say that I looked at other people as being *smaller*; rather, I recognized that I was willing to go *all in* while others were happier to conform to norms...to accept what they already had as good enough.

What if you were ready right now to be the visionary leader and speaker I believe you arrived into this world as?

What if all your dreams and visions were, in fact, possible?

Would you be willing to consider that adopting an unapologetic stance for who you are and what you believe is the road to bringing your dreams and visions to life?

## YOU ARE READY, NOW

I believe (and know) you are already ready—that you should go out and deliver your vision, and share your dreams, desires, and beliefs. They and you are ready to be unleashed!

You are ready to be unashamed and to celebrate the truth that you are unbroken and unbreakable.

You are ready to be unquiet—unchained from comparanoia and any inkling that you are unloved in this world.

You are ready to be unafraid and unmessable by others—unwavering in the way you show up as *you* in this world.

You are ready to get uncorked and to celebrate who you are—to celebrate that you are already unboring and that you already possess qualities that make you unforgettable.

You are ready to be unconventional, unorthodox even, sometimes unreasonable, and radically unstoppable when it comes to who you are, what you believe for others, and your vision for greatness in this world.

You are ready to stop measuring yourself against the value you deliver and to start delivering your vision—and people will recognize and celebrate you as an unbeatable force.

You are ready to pave the road that is your truth—the road back to who you truly are.

You are ready to celebrate you!

What is the most powerful next step you will take?

_____

_____

_____

Who are you celebrating right now? Write a letter to yourself that celebrates who you are and the road you are paving to fulfill your miracle and your destiny.

_____

_____

_____

_____

# BEING UNSTOPPABLE

Signature _____ Date _____

# SPOTLIGHT: UNAPOLOGETIC INFLUENCER

## UNAPOLOGETIC
### BY LAKEISHA MICHELLE

*LaKeisha Michelle is a singer, speaker, and creator. You can learn more about her at LaKeishaMichelle.com.*

Unforgettable! I love when Maya Angelou said people never forget how you make them feel. I commit most to leaving the highest energy to those who come in contact with me in any venture I may have! I never want people to forget that love, joy, peace, giving, possibility, and abundance are all their birthright. I want people to remember that being themselves is enough, and that there is a magic that just happens when you simply shine.

For me, being unapologetic means I am no longer shrinking. I am no longer sorry for my decisions. I am no longer feeling as though I am in the way. I am who I am. I trust and know my heart and intentions are good, so I don't have to over-/under-compensate to make others feel comfortable.

More than ten years ago, I was in an abusive relationship. Part of why I stayed, I told myself, was because I felt bad! I actually was worried about all the crap he cried about and I felt sorry for him. I thought he "needed me," as if I were a shrink or something. *Please*. The good news is I decided I was willing to die for my freedom. As I am writing this, I'm not dead, and today, I am free as hell (if that's a thing), and I travel the world. I work from wherever and daily create life on my terms! Side note: I have a hot, happy man who is the ultimate gentleman as well! I realized what real love looked like and moved the heck on unapologetically!

Growing up as a young woman, I was told to cover up. I was told my butt was too big, and that I needed to be seen not heard. I was told to sing only gospel, and that ladies are to make the home while the hubby brings home the bacon. I was told my name was ghetto, and that if I wanted people to hire me, I should use Michelle and not LaKeisha. I was told no makeup, no hair weaves, and certainly no nail designs or nail polish.

Oh, my God! I would be in church with a wrinkled nose wondering where they were getting this crock of poo! While I love God to this day and am actually super-spiritual, I realized that people create rules...and worse, other people actually follow them without testing them out and listening to what their hearts and souls resonate with! (Obviously, I always got in trouble for questioning what I was being told. They even called me Jezzy...short for Jezebel!)

When I entered the real world, I was confused at first because I didn't know what was real anymore. I was so afraid of going "too far" and disappointing my family, so I spun in circles doing a lot of things that looked cool but weren't my true calling.

I decided to search out what my heart was telling me to be true. I know that finding purpose is a life's journey, and I am on it.

I just got back from San Diego sharing my message in song and conversation on stage to more than 1,000 people about how I am daily deleting old rules and writing new ones of my own. I think you should too.

I am grateful for those past rules, and the people who handed them to me. We learn from others what they are taught, and whether they are good or bad, I believe our experiences *all* work out for our good.

It wasn't until I realized I was not responsible for anyone else's happiness that I finally started living. I released what people might think as I explored and tried new things. If I failed okay, but at least I would die empty, having tried all that was inside of me.

Being unapologetic allows me to fully embrace my gifts and urgently share them so others are inspired and give themselves permission to do the same. Being unapologetic means I am retracing the rules I've been taught to live by, and if they no longer fit where I am going, I unapologetically release them with ease and write the new script.

Every second of your day makes up your life. Don't just go along with things to appease others. Realize that those who dare to challenge the status quo are all we talk about years and decades after they are gone from this earth.

Choose to be relentless in going after what you know is yours. One of my favorite stories is that of Jabez, a kid whose entire family wrote him off. He went against his circumstances and decided to be different, to stand out, even to look crazy, and not to subscribe to what his family prescribed! He simply prayed a sentence-long prayer in total faith for an unrecognizable, amazing, expanded life. God granted his request.

I don't know about you, but I am willing to be unapologetic about my future. I am open to receive all that belongs to me. I choose to shine bright, and as Lisa Nichols says, "If they don't like it, tell them to put on some shades." I am no longer dimming my light for the sake of someone else. *Shine* bright, darling, and *be* unapologetic.

# CELEBRATION
## WHAT ARE YOU CELEBRATING RIGHT NOW?

**UN** ARE YOU READY TO BE
UNAPOLOGETIC?

# A FINAL NOTE
## WHO ARE YOU BEING?

UNBROKEN
UNCHAINED
UNAFRAID UNCORKED
UNQUIET
UNREASONABLE UNLOVED
UNFORGETTABLE
UNBEATABLE
UNBORING
UNMESSABLE
UNORTHODOX
UNBURDENED
UNBREAKABLE
UNWAVERING
UNSTOPPABLE
UNCONVENTIONAL
UNLEASHED
UNAPOLOGETIC

Now that you've finished this book, what are you going to do? More importantly, who will you be committed to being as you execute the action steps you identify as those that will bring you closer to becoming the visionary leader and speaker I know you are? What is the most powerful next step you will take? Who will you choose to be in the face of adversity? Who will you choose to be when you wake up every morning? Who will you align yourself with? Who will you choose as a mentor and guide? What and how will you celebrate your everyday extraordinary life as you journey toward achieving your mission and vision?

Above all else, I now challenge you to commit to being the person you want to be. I challenge you to apply all the wisdom, knowledge, and action steps I gave you in this book. I challenge you to commit to making celebration a habit as opposed to a luxury. I invite you to celebrate the good, the bad, and the ugly—to recognize every moment as extraordinary and to celebrate both physically (yes, with *asstitude*) and mentally every day, multiple times per day.

Take a pen or a pencil, right now. In the lines below, declare who you are going to be moving forward. Maybe you'll commit to taking on an unapologetic stance, or maybe you'll commit to being more *unmessable* by outside circumstances. Whatever you declare, choose attributes that are not already things you normally are. Stretch yourself and the vision you have for yourself.

Declare it.

For the next ninety days, I'm going to be:

_____

_____

_____

_____

Now, what are the ten most potent actions you will commit to over the next ninety days? Perhaps it's a new morning routine (be specific). Maybe you'll adopt my method of setting the phone timer for five to ten times per day to celebrate. Or maybe you'll decide to have some clarifying conversations with family, friends, or business associates.

Write the ten most potent actions you will commit to taking over the next ninety days:

_____

_____

_____

_____

_____

_____

_____

# A FINAL NOTE

In this book, you discovered the truth about yourself as you identified the breadcrumbs of your life. You began to accept and celebrate who you already are and how to go *all in* on your dreams and vision. You developed the confidence and critical thinking skills to allow you to take a stand for what you believe. You learned how to *be* a visionary leader and speaker who effortlessly enrolls others through story. You learned how to share your gifts with the world and to lead others with vision instead of playing the *value game*. You learned to be a confident leader in the leading role of your own life and as an influencer of those who follow you.

I've taught you how to uncover and unleash the X Factor that will allow you to achieve your mission and vision just like the world's greatest personalities, leaders, and luminaries!

If you stay committed to being unapologetic in who you are, unapologetic in your drive for greatness, and unwavering in your commitment to staying accountable to the action steps you've set out for yourself, you will move exponentially closer to becoming the leader and visionary you see yourself as, and you will do it much faster than you could have ever imagined.

Now that you've completed being unapologetic, please contact me to let me know what you loved and what you'd love to see more of in the next edition of this book. Most importantly, I'd love to hear where you're at in your journey of being unapologetic. Share your celebrations and your challenges (that I know you'll celebrate, too). Tell me how I can support you to become the visionary speaker and leader your followers are waiting for. Let's book a call, or better yet, maybe you can book me to speak to your organization, school, clients, or community.

I'd love to offer you a no-obligation, complimentary 30-60 minute consultation to support you in achieving your speaking and leadership goals. My email address is Davide@BeingUnapologetic.com; however, I encourage you to text me on my personal cell phone at (619) 363.0568. Be sure to include your name and your time zone so we can coordinate your complimentary consultation.

What are you waiting for?

I hope I've inspired you not to make the same mistake I did when I was in the first grade, waiting for hours for my brother to pick me up from the schoolyard.

I hope you're inspired not to make the same mistake I did by waiting until I was thirty-three to have an honest conversation with my biological family.

I hope you recognize, now, that you've arrived into this world ready to create miracles for others. To speak, lead, and inspire great transformation and be the example for others to celebrate the miracles they possess, too.

When I speak to audiences, I always say, "Over my dead body will you exit this world without the same standing ovation you arrived with." This book is my legacy to ensure that even after I'm gone, you will be reminded to embrace your destiny by stepping into the spotlight—the spotlight that was cast upon you the moment you arrived, and the one you deserve not only to be in, but to confidently cast on others who are waiting for the message and leadership only you can deliver.

So take your Disney-sized dreams, your ideas that seem as impossible as landing on Mars, and all your everyday extraordinary stories and experiences. Take your imagination, your breath, and your *being*, and stand up, speak out, and be unapologetic. Then you will inspire and lead others to also step into the spotlight of their own miracles.

The world is waiting for you.

You're ready now to be unapologetic!

"You're ready now to be unapologetic."

— Davide Di Giorgio

# ABOUT THE AUTHOR

Davide Di Giorgio is an international best-selling author, keynote speaker, TEDx speaker, youth ambassador, and speaking and confidence consultant for influencers and celebrities.

Davide is also an award-winning theater producer, composer, and acclaimed educator. His work and message have been featured around the world on podcasts, radio, and national media.

He is a contributing author in *Reach Your Greatness* and the *Better Business Book*, and a featured writer for *The Good Men Project*, *Thought Catalog*, *Thrive Global*, *Life By Design Magazine*, and *Success Profiles Magazine*.

He's on a mission to empower everyday extraordinary individuals, especially young people, to compare less and celebrate more. His philanthropic endeavor, *Project Being Unapologetic* dares to tackle bullying and build confidence and self-esteem while funding dream projects for high school performing arts students.

Originally from Toronto, when he's not traveling around the world speaking or enjoying a dream trip, Davide now lives in his dream city, San Diego.

Connect with Davide at:
BeingUNapologetic.com

Subscribe to Davide's YouTube Channel:
BeingUNapologeticTV.com

# PROJECT BEING UNAPOLOGETIC

Everyone has a story about being bullied and not feeling like they could fully be themselves.

Project Being Unapologetic dares to tackle the issue of bullying for high school students and their teachers while instilling confidence and the essence of Being Unapologetic as a way to be empowered to become a visionary leader. Launched in 2018 on Davide's forty-second birthday, Project Being Unapologetic is a twenty-five-plus-year passion project and his life's work.

Performing Arts programs around the world attract students who sometimes don't feel like they fit in. The arts are a place of safety that allow for true expression. Teachers of the arts often become counselors and friends. It was the performing arts that changed and saved Davide's life when he was in high school.

The program launched in March of 2018 with the Ruben S. Ayala High School Choir from Chino Hills, California. Teacher Robert Davis was referred to Davide when he put a call out on Facebook for a deserving performing arts program. When Robert Davis asked his students what they wanted most for their program, they answered *respect*. The $5,000 they received went to a choral commission. A composer is writing a piece for the choir that it will get to premiere in 2019. See what happened that day at ProjectUNx.com.

Every copy of *Being Unapologetic* supports a performing arts high school program. Davide is also going after big corporate and celebrity endorsements. If you know anyone who'd love the project and the vision to take it around the country and the world to inspire students and teachers while funding their dream projects, please connect us.

ProjectUNx@BeingUnapologetic.com
ProjectUNx.com
Help us to take this project viral so we can empower millions and fund dream projects around the world.

# SPEAKER AND INFLUENCER COACHING

If you want to be hired as a professional speaker (one who gets paid), your focus needs to be on marketing yourself and being unapologetic about it.

Your celebrity speaking and influencer marketing platform, designed to let meeting planners and event coordinators know you are their best choice, includes:

- A brand platform and positioning that speaks to planners and influencers in your industry
- A website with a speaking page strategically branded for you as a professional speaker
- A media one-sheet and professional speaker kit/electronic press kit
- A speaker bio (there are at least three kinds of bios you need to have ready)
- Speaker headshot and speaking shots
- Social media accounts optimized for a professional speaker
- A social media strategy that attracts speaking opportunities, loyal followers, and paying coaching/consulting clients
- A speaker trailer/sizzle reel (it doesn't have to break the bank, and is easier to complete than you may think)
- A book or other published works that position you as an expert
- Your story and idea worth spreading (that you can share in as little as a few seconds)

To learn how to unleash your celebrity speaking and influencer platform, contact Davide for a complimentary consultation:

Davide@BeingUnapologetic.com
(619) 363.0568

# BEING UNAPOLOGETIC EXPERIENCES

Being Unapologetic Experiences are uniquely immersive mansion, resort, adventure, and cruise experiences where you will get direct access to Davide and his inner circle and get to mastermind with other on-purpose influencers and speakers. Opportunities include:

- Masterminding with other high achieving experts, speakers, authors, and on-purpose leaders as you explore world-class destinations.
- Discovering new solutions and opportunities for exponentially growing your business; forging joint-venture relationships and new alliances.
- Receiving group coaching and mentorship to develop and exponentially grow your vision and business.
- Enjoying unprecedented networking opportunities with Davide's inner circle of experts and advisors.

Contact Davide to learn more and to apply for upcoming Being Unapologetic Experiences:

Davide@BeingUnapologetic.com

(619) 363.0568

# ADDITIONAL RESOURCES

To help you achieve even more success,

**Get Your FREE BONUS RESOURCES at:**

FreeGiftFromDavide.com

**Subscribe to Davide on YouTube at:**

BeingUnapologeticTV.com

**Join Davide's FREE UNetwork Community for Speakers and Leaders at:**

UnapologeticSpeakers.com

**Join Davide's Travel Lovers Tribe Community at:**

TravelLoversTribe.com

**Follow Davide's Daily Adventures on Instagram:**

@BeingUnapologetic.com

**Ready to Compare Less, Celebrate More?:**

123Celebrate.com

**Access The Resources, Products, Tools, and Toys Davide Uses and Loves at:**

UNbasics.com

# BOOK DAVIDE TO SPEAK

Davide Di Giorgio is not your everyday speaker. He turns speaking engagements into immersive experiences that will not only entertain and educate your audience members, but leave them transformed.

He's spent more than twenty-five years working with performers, presenters, speakers, and leaders across multiple industries from performance to personal development, travel to transformation, and education to entrepreneurship and executive leadership.

Davide speaks on the power of using celebration as the anecdote to what he calls comparanoia, building unmessable confidence, visionary leadership, and unlocking disruptive speaking and storytelling.

His talks are customized for corporate, entrepreneurial, and educational (educator and student) audiences.

For corporate engagements, learn how Davide also includes the opportunity for you to give back to a local high school performing arts program of your choice that he will speak to and surprise with a portion of his speaking fee.

Contact Davide directly to inquire about customizing a talk for your event or organization.

BeingUnapologetic.com
RFQ@BeingUnapologetic.com
(619) 363.0568

www.ingramcontent.com/pod-product-compliance
Lightning Source LLC
Chambersburg PA
CBHW052053110526
44591CB00013B/2192